RULE YOUR AUTHOR EMPIRE

THE STEP-BY-STEP PLAN TO TAKE CONTROL OF YOUR WRITING CAREER

K. CARPENTER

PRAISE FOR RULE YOUR AUTHOR EMPIRE

"It's the cure for author overwhelm."

- Bestselling Author and Renowned Business Coach Heather Hildenbrand

"This is a must-read for newer/intermediate authors. I absolutely LOVED it! As an author who's now starting over, I found this to be an invaluable read. It was like K. Carpenter was speaking directly to me. I really appreciate how the book felt like a conversation, almost like we were having coffee and she was generously sharing everything she knew about publishing. I flew through the pages because it was so engaging! This book was instrumental in helping me refine my long-term publishing strategy which is game-changing! And there are even more ideas that I will come back to to grow my business even further. What a great resource! I highly recommend Rule Your Author Empire!"

- Author Mandy Michaels

"The "what not to spend money on" email? Fantastic. I wish someone would have told me half this shit 5 years ago."

- Annie Anderson on the *Rule Your Author Empire* newsletter

CHAPTER 1
INTRODUCTION

I wrote this book for the authors crying, banging their heads on the desk, and asking the universe what they're doing wrong. I hate that, and I never want that to be you. What I want doesn't matter though, this book is about what you want and what you're willing to do to get it.

- Are you a 4- or 5-figure author striving to get to 6 figures?
- Are you exhausted from trying to write more with every spare minute, just to see the same income on your dashboard?
- Do you feel like you're stuck on a plateau, looking around for whatever

secret door will help you level up your author career?

If so, I've got good news for you. You, my dear reader, are the author I wrote this for. In this book you will learn:

1. My *1 Year to 6 Figures* plan to help you **sell more books with less effort**.
2. How to discern what you're wasting time on so that you can **get your life back**.

Being a writer means you write. You write until the story is told. Being an author...now that's a different ballgame—and one that I'm all too familiar with. If that draft is done and you're sitting there asking yourself "now what?" that's where I can provide some insight.

I'm Kel Carpenter, a fantasy romance author earning *nearly half a million dollars per year* from my books.

What's more, I only work from 9:00–4:00 five days a week (and constantly have my schedule disrupted with appointments for the kiddo). I only spend three days a week writing; the other two are for admin and marketing. I don't work weekends.

What is *your* writing schedule like? Does this sound too good to be true? I've got good news for you: I've been where you are now, and I can help you get to where you want to be: writing and making full-time money from it.

We'll walk through publishing YOUR books, step by step, and at the end of this journey you'll know *exactly* what you need to do to make 6 figures a year.

1 YEAR TO 6 FIGURES

1 Year to 6 Figures is a plan that I created after breaking down the aspects that are most important in an author's empire. Through this, we will evaluate your product, your branding, your marketing, where you should be publishing, and ways to achieve longevity in your writing career.

Sounds simple, right? That's because it is.

Facebook and other social media platforms have convinced authors that you need to do everything, all the time, to succeed. The reality is: that's blatantly untrue. I don't mean to imply those people are lying to you, just that perhaps they haven't been able to take a step back and see the broader picture for themselves. It is harder to see the forest through the trees.

Rule Your Author Empire will teach you what steps you need to take to level up your author career and make over $100,000 a year, while also showing you which steps you can ignore for now, because not everything moves the needle.

No longer will you be staying up late to write (unless that's your regular time by choice) or missing your kiddo's dance recital to meet impossible deadlines. You'll stop losing sleep and start making more money while you sleep. Through my comprehensive breakdown and subsequent plan, I will give you homework to help you map out the best steps you can personally take to help grow your income into a stable author career.

If you're the type that likes keeping assignments all in one place, you might want to check out my workbook. You get it as a free download if you join my newsletter at RuleYourAuthorEmpire.com.

I'VE BEEN WHERE YOU ARE NOW

How do I know this plan works? Because I've been where you are. I've ridden the highs and lows of instability that comes from having windfall income, which is what we all have as authors. Three months after my son was born, I was back to work and writing every single day for two months to meet a deadline I never should have set, all because I was scared that my income would drop if that book wasn't out on time. It had before. What reason could I possibly have to believe it wouldn't now?

The truth is, there were several problems at play here. The first was my own insecurities and anxiety because I didn't have a plan. After all, you reap what you sow, and I hadn't prepared the right way for having a baby or the time off I would need during my journey into motherhood.

Another thing is the values that are often instilled in author groups on Facebook and blogs. "Hard works pays off," they say. *But if that were really true, wouldn't you be a 6-figure author already?*

You're posting on TikTok every day, sending out newsletters every week, crafting the perfect author Instagram, and releasing every three months so you "stay relevant." You're doing all ninety-nine things that "they" say you need to do, but you're still not a 6-figure author. So clearly the problem isn't how hard you're working, it's something else.

The good news is that I am you. I have

been there, pulling my hair out, crying because I was so stressed and the words wouldn't come, feeling the pressure of my bank account like the hounds of hell coming for me. It might sound dramatic, but it's a real feeling and it sucks.

LIVING YOUR BEST AUTHOR LIFE

Now you're probably thinking, *"Kel, why the heck is that good news?"*

Because, friend, now I'm living my best life. I'm a financially stable author making a healthy 6 figures through a variety of means. My books have been translated into four languages. I have audiobooks with big publishers. I've hit the *USA Today* list and sold over half a million books.

I don't stay up late to write or edit anymore. I don't work on the weekends. I've left my workaholic, insecure self behind to live my best life and *you can, too.*

- Bestseller lists? They're within your reach.
- Selling hundreds of thousands of books? You got this.

- Foreign publishers want your books? They sure as hell do, they just don't know it yet.

You have to show them, and if you're wondering how on earth you can do that, I've got you.

CHAPTER 2
MINDSET MATTERS

We have to start here because mindset is the most important thing. Whether you're a beginner or have been publishing for years, your mindset will always matter. It's the true difference in who withstands the test of time in this roller coaster industry.

SUCCESS IS THE ONLY OPTION

My journey started when I was fifteen years old. My family couldn't afford to buy books at the rate I was reading. So, I decided to write my own. By sixteen, I had a finished manuscript. Like many of you, I queried agents and even had a few requests for my full draft. In the end, no one picked up the manuscript and I set it aside for five years.

When I was twenty, I read a book that was self-published and loved it. This was the first time I'd read a self-published author (that I knew of). Reading her book made me start to think that maybe, just maybe, I could self-publish, too.

My author career started at that moment. Before that, I was simply a writer, but now? Now I was thinking about entering the game.

My motto was, "success is the only option." Pretty vague, huh? The reality is, whatever my definition of success was at the time, I was still aiming for *something*. That manuscript ended up needing months with the editor and I had to save up tips for seven months from the pizza gig I was working to pay for it. Was it hard? Yes, but in the end, I had a book ready to go and a cover that was passable.

I published on my twenty-first birthday. Did I make millions my first year? God, no. My debut launched and made $50 its first month. And guess what? I was disappointed, but I didn't give up. I did a promotion for $40 its second month and made $150. It was an improvement, but still not where I wanted to be.

So, I got some feedback on my product and learned my cover wasn't up to snuff. That third month I paid a professional designer to create the cover of my dreams. I literally cried, y'all. The day I uploaded that new cover, my sales more than tripled overnight.

That book made $3,000 in its third month. Then again in its fourth, and once more in its fifth. Now that's what I'm talking about. My debut series has gone on to sell over 100,000 copies. It's translated into Portuguese, French, and German. The audiobooks alone make a healthy five figures a year to this day.

Does that sound successful to you? Success is different to everyone. It isn't quantifiable. It's determined by whatever *you* think it is. For me, I was on my way to building the career of my dreams.

"WHETHER YOU THINK YOU CAN, OR YOU THINK YOU CAN'T— YOU'RE RIGHT." — HENRY FORD

This statement from Henry Ford is so simple, but profoundly true. Yes, you can't start out and expect that you're going to make a million dollars in your first year. I mean you can, but if believing it was all it took, we'd all be millionaires. Right?

However, if you plan for success, whatever way you want to define it, I guarantee that you'll do better than if you hadn't. If you believe that you can't, the plans you make will be full of doubt. You will sabotage yourself and your career.

LET ME PUT THIS ANOTHER WAY.

I felt I had to do some soul searching and took a deep dive into the world of manifestation. I started with Heather Hildenbrand's book, *Manifest Your HEA*. The thing that sold me? Well, the title was a good start. The idea that I could manifest my own happily ever after, or otherwise think my way into living my best life—sign me the hell up! I think most of us would feel that way if it were that simple.

Spoiler alert: It's not.

When I started *Manifest Your HEA*, I was more than a little dubious—and if you're anything like me, the word "manifest" is basically synonymous with *woo-woo*. That's not what I took away from the book, however. Instead of indoctrinating me into a cult of woo, this book taught me that reshaping my thinking is reshaping my world. And here's the kicker—it worked.

I went on to do coaching with Heather and one of the things she told me felt so utterly profound

I'm compelled to share it. She said that in many ways, success is a ladder. It's not a black-and-white absolute.

We don't have success—or not.

We *are* being successful. We are working toward our desired outcome.

If I want to be a million-dollar author, then I need to believe I can be one. Part of that is shifting my perspective, and part of it is watching it happen in reality as I shift with it.

Each rung of the ladder is the next step that takes me closer and closer to my goal. So instead of telling myself I am a failure because I'm not there yet, I say that I am *becoming* a seven-figure author. Just as *you* are becoming a 6-figure author.

My reality is what I've chosen to make it through the work I've done to better myself, and it will continue to improve because I choose to. I wake up and make the choice every day to strive for that next rung on the ladder to seven figures.

DO YOU UNDERSTAND?

At its core, the mindset you need to remember is that the universe is going to deliver to you what you believe and plan for. My husband likes to say, "God helps those that help themselves." Whether you believe in a higher power or not, the sentiment is still true. You must take the steps to reach for six figures if you want to make it.

If you'd like to work on your mindset while moving through *Rule Your Author Empire*, I suggest *Write to Riches* by Renee Rose in addition to *Manifest Your HEA* by Heather Hildenbrand. Both are fabulous guides to help you better yourself from your couch.

Now you say, *"But Kel, it really isn't that simple, is it?"*

The reality of making millions of dollars in one year from ground zero probably isn't, but **the mindset that will get you to six figures is 100% that simple.**

We start here because this mindset is the singular thing you need beyond a finished manuscript to begin the *1 Year to 6 Figures* plan. If you believe you can, you will.

Are you ready to dive in? Let's begin.

CHAPTER 3
1 YEAR TO 6 FIGURES

The following five steps are the heart of the *1 Year to 6 Figures* plan. These are the core pillars that go into building both a kingdom and your author empire— the metaphorical structures and roads and towns— needed to grow your fortune. These steps will help you assess your own books and platform and successfully create or adapt your plan.

STEP ONE: LAYING THE FOUNDATION FOR YOUR AUTHOR EMPIRE

The foundation of any house, kingdom, or author empire (in our case), is the single most important factor. If you want a solid author career, you need a solid foundation. That's why the first step is assessing which way you publish and why. Whether you've got a hundred books out or are preparing your debut, this step is absolutely crucial.

In this step, we will cover where you publish and the why it's a strategic decision in making six figures:

- Self-Publishing Options
- Kindle Unlimited — Will you be in Kindle Unlimited, and exclusive to Amazon by extension?
- Wide — Will you publish "wide" and try to get your book in as many places as possible?
- Hybrid — Will you publish in **both** Kindle Unlimited and wide?

Which route do you want to take? This is just a small taste of what awaits in this chapter, and the answers to these questions can decide where you should publish and define your career.

STEP TWO: BUILDING THE FRAMEWORK OF YOUR AUTHOR EMPIRE

You've laid your foundation. Now it's time to put up the framework. This is your product, aka, books. In this step, we will evaluate your product to make sure it's 6-figure worthy by breaking it down into the following categories:

- Cover
- Blurb
- Reviews
- Look Inside

Without going into craft, these are the main components that decide if your book is marketable. Readers will judge a book by its cover; this is known. But they also read the blurb to decide if it sounds interesting to them, and if they're a particularly discerning reader, they'll read your reviews. You can't control your reviews, but you can control the other moving parts.

This section is all about putting your best foot forward in the literary sense and how to spot if one of these issues may be failing you.

Hint — if you're not to six figures yet, there is a really good chance that this is part of the problem!

STEP THREE: DECKING OUT YOUR AUTHOR EMPIRE

You've got your foundation, you've built the framework, now it's time to deck it out! By this, I mean adding insulation, creating walls, wiring the whole establishment, and everything that goes into making a building a complete space.

In other, more authorly words, this is your branding.

You might think of pretty social media posts or an author logo when I say branding, and those are part of it, but there's also so much more. How do you paint a picture of you as a successful author? This section focuses on:

- Branding: You are defined by your brand. What do I mean by this?
- Looking at my brand: Kindle Unlimited, Wide, KU to Wide
- Time to talk about the "T" word: Tropes. Also, Butter.

- The devil is in the details. *Hint* — it's about the *how*, not the
- what.
- Social media
- Coauthor branding
- Where the land meets the sea, aka, writing to market.

Branding is everything that you put out to readers. Every post, every book, every graphic. With how much it encompasses, it's no wonder that so many authors don't really understand or know what their branding is. If you fall into that category, the good news for you is: I did, too. Which means I can tell you how to better unify your branding so that you can grow your core audience.

STEP FOUR: PAVING THE ROADS TO YOUR AUTHOR EMPIRE

We've laid the foundation, built the framework, and decked it out. This is fabulous, because now it's time for my favorite thing to discuss—and the bane of so many authors—marketing.

You can write the best book in the world, but if you don't market it, not a single soul will know it exists and you'll fall into the dreaded abyss that is Amazon. If you want to earn six figures and more from your books, you'll need to know:

- Different types of marketing: passive versus active
- Facebook advertising
- The downsides of when you market poorly
- How to best utilize social media to make six figures
- The differences in marketing wide vs in Kindle Unlimited
- Selling direct
- Coauthor marketing

My goal for you is to pave the roads for your readers to find your books, and become part of your author empire. To do this, we'll go through the sections listed above and more, so that when you finish this chapter, you know *exactly* how to best market your books.

STEP FIVE: CRAFTING THE LEGEND OF YOUR AUTHOR EMPIRE

You've built out your author empire. There are structures and roads and towns—all the things you need to make an author empire. Your books. Your brand. Your marketing. The last step is to craft the legend that is YOU.

Combine these things and you'll find a way to forge forward into six figures. But when you're done and want to look beyond your borders to start attracting new readers, that's where working on *longevity* helps. Some of the things we'll cover in this section are:

- Series versus standalones
- Coauthoring
- Boxsets
- Shared worlds
- Kickstarter
- The importance of having a backlist
- Formats: audiobooks, translations, and print
- Burnout

My goal for this final step is that you're able to

go out into the wild west that is publishing and successfully *RULE YOUR AUTHOR EMPIRE*. That title is starting to make more sense now, isn't it?

If you're feeling excited and ready to go, that's great. Hold on to that energy and mindset because, like I said previously, your mindset is the single most important thing.

I can teach you everything I know, but just like I can lead a horse to water, I can't make it drink, and I can't make you apply everything you'll learn in this book. To do that, you'll have to approach your career without rose-tinted glasses and be willing to get down into the dirt. After all, the only person who can do it is you. It may seem hard at times, but I've got you. We can do this.

CHAPTER 4
LAYING THE FOUNDATION

Let's start with the basics of *where* you're publishing.

The way I see it, you have three options: traditional publishing, self-publishing in Kindle Unlimited, and self-publishing "wide."

I can't help you with traditional publishing. You need to query agents and have a pre-edited manuscript. That is the best advice I can give. That, and don't give up. All it takes is one yes. So if that's your route, then take it and *own* it.

While this book isn't written with traditional publishing in mind, I do believe there are valuable insights to be gained for all publishing options, particularly in the areas of branding, marketing, and longevity. We've got a good bit to cover to keep you on track with your 6-figure journey.

SELF-PUBLISHING OPTIONS

There are two main ways to self-publish and they are *radically* different from one another.

1. **Publishing in Kindle Unlimited** — This is a program Amazon offers where, in exchange for being exclusive to them, your book can be downloaded and earn page reads. Pages are worth a certain amount, and you're paid based on the pages read. That amount is calculated from an overall pot of money from all the KU subscriptions pooled together, then divided by the total pages read across the platform. At least, this is as much as authors can put together from what Amazon has said. They are not the most transparent with their system, so there is some guesswork involved.

2. **Publishing "Wide"** — This means publishing widely across many platforms which can include, but isn't limited to: Apple, Amazon, Barnes and Noble, Kobo, Google Play, Scribd, and Tolino. You may also choose to sell directly

through your own website, use a subscription-style platform like Patreon and/or Ream, or on apps like Radish and Dreame. Publishing wide lets you get your books to as many retailers as possible, but **you can't put your book in KU and be wide**. You have to choose.

Let's take a deeper look at these two options and why someone might go one way versus the other.

KINDLE UNLIMITED

Kindle Unlimited, also known as KU, focuses heavily on rank. For our purposes, rank is *the number at which your book is ranked in Amazon's system*. Now, being in KU automatically gives you a boost because both borrows (books downloaded through KU) and purchases (books purchased at full price) count towards your rank.

It's well known that a higher rank is easier to achieve in the first ninety days after publishing. That's considered the rough estimate of when you'll see your rank start to fall if your book isn't sticky.

"Sticky" means maintaining a high rank without having to push heavily through advertising methods.

I know this is a lot to take in if you're newer, but stick (get it?) with me. This information is super important because if rank and page reads go hand in hand, it stands to reason that those who publish *quickly* will benefit more from this program.

How it works

The way you make money in Kindle Unlimited is through something called **page reads**. Amazon has developed a system to be able to tell how far a reader reads in a book. Those pages read are assigned a value, and that's how authors are paid for their books. The page-read value changes every month and goes up and down because it is a base amount determined by the overall pool of KU subscriptions. For this reason, KU also heavily favors long books instead of short ones because the longer the book, the more pages read.

Monogamy

One very notable thing about this system is that you must be *exclusive* to Amazon to participate in the program, which means your books cannot be published in e-format *anywhere* else. Amazon takes this rule very seriously and has banned accounts that have broken it, even if the book was pirated and it wasn't actually the author's fault.

Risky Choices? Maybe.

Because of this, there is a certain amount of risk involved in being in Kindle Unlimited. You have to put all your eggs, or books, in one basket and hope that no one takes your basket, kicks it over, or steals your eggs. This can be nerve-racking for many people, but it's often considered the lesser evil for authors that choose to be in KU. Why is that?

Going wide requires more time. You have to put in a significant number of hours up-front when you are uploading your books to multiple retailers. Amazon is a one-and-done kind of deal. But wide? You're uploading everywhere and then promoting everywhere. In many ways KU is easier, but it's undoubtedly higher risk.

WIDE

This way of publishing means you can publish your book anywhere and everywhere. The main retailers people publish at are Apple, Amazon, Kobo, Google Play, and Barnes and Noble. You can publish many more places through a third-party system called Draft2Digital, but they will take a 10% cut of the royalties to do so.

You can also publish on subscription platforms like Ream, Radish, Dreame, and Galatea. These platforms can be big moneymakers depending on what you write as they primarily favor spicy romance.

Lastly, you can sell directly to your reader through your website or a more personalized subscription platform like Patreon.

Bank Before Rank

Wide books focus on the bank before rank mentality, or in other words, prioritizing money earned over popularity. Your rank at places like Amazon will often be worse than if it were in Kindle Unlimited, but it has no bearing on how much you're making the way it does in Kindle Unlimited, because you're making money from many different platforms instead of just one.

Another benefit is that because you're no longer rank-dependent. This option appeals to people who need more flexibility in their publishing schedule. So, if you write "slower," i.e. fewer than roughly four books a year, this might be a better option.

There's fewer mountains and valleys

This means you won't have the huge windfall

income that can come from being in KU during releases, but you're less susceptible to your income being cut by more than half from month to month. This makes publishing wide a great option for those that value consistency and need or want less risk involved. You'll experience a slower build that remains more consistent over time.

Time = Money

Because the readers wide are used to paying full price, shorter books are a positive. You make the same as longer ones if the price tag is the same. Consequently, longer books can be a downside when going wide because there's no obvious perk to writing more and making the same as someone who wrote a shorter novel. Particularly if the time spent could have yielded two or more novels instead. Readers obviously still like longer books, but they're far from necessary with this method of publishing.

Selling Direct

One notable thing I want to stress in publishing wide is the ability to sell directly to your reader through your own website. This allows readers to buy directly from you without going through Amazon, Apple, Kobo, etc. Doing this made a huge difference in my income. Being able to cut out the middleman means *keeping all your profits*. There's nothing sweeter than getting 100% of your royalties. I'll go into this more in the marketing chapter.

These are just some of the benefits to publishing wide, but remember, you will have more setup and more maintenance. Every platform has its own promotions and ways that you can apply to them. Running ads is one of the main ways to get more visibility and can be more of a time suck if you try to prioritize them by platform.

That said, those with a low risk tolerance will most likely love wide over KU any day, even if it's more work. You have eggs in every basket so if someone steals one, kicks it over, or takes an egg—it's not as big a problem.

HYBRID

This model utilizes *both* Kindle Unlimited *and* Wide, and is actually the model I, myself, use. For me, 90% of my books are wide while the remaining 10% are in Kindle Unlimited.

"All right, but Kel, how did you come to this decision when you proposed it as a one-or-the-other sort of thing?"

Because, dear reader, I have been wanting to be fully wide for years now, but I'm still in the transitioning phase. About three years ago, I moved one series wide, then six months later I moved another. For the past three years I've moved one or two series a year wide until only my newest releases are available in Kindle Unlimited.

Why is that? you might ask.

Two reasons.

1. I write longer books now than I used to, and longer books = more page reads.
2. I got my start in KU and don't want to lose that readership. It helps that I write in very KU-heavy genres as well (paranormal romance and reverse harem).

For the past two years, I've kept releasing into KU, while pulling my backlist wide one series at a time. This lets me get the higher highs of releasing into KU while maintaining stability with my wide income.

My long-term goal is to be fully wide, and hybrid publishing is a great way to get there so that you don't crash your income if you've been KU dependent up to this point. I recommend using the strategy I went with, where I pulled my lowest-performing series first out of Kindle

Unlimited because it would cost the least amount to my bottom line while giving me somewhere to start.

Even if your goal isn't to transition, but to be hybrid long term, this is a great way to go about it. Some series perform great in KU, some perform great wide, others perform well no matter which way you go. The only way you will know how your series will perform is picking a way and trying it. Worst case: You go the other direction with it later, once the data suggests that your approach isn't working.

The beautiful thing about self-publishing is nothing is permanent. In the words of author Elana Johnson, "YOU are the boss." You have the power to decide which path you want to take, and to double back and try the other one if it doesn't work out.

SO, WHICH ROUTE DO YOU TAKE?

Let's review questions to ask yourself when deciding which publishing option to take. There's a graphic in the workbook that will help you to decide. You can download through my newsletter which you can join at RuleYourAuthorEmpire.com.

- Do you write fast and publish a book a month? Or do you write slower, like one book a year?
- Do you write long books that would benefit from a system based on page reads? Or shorter ones that would do better making a flat amount?
- Are you someone that likes a little risk in life? Or are you risk averse?
- Would you rather have consistency, or more extreme highs, even if they come with lows?
- Does the ease of being on one platform outweigh the benefits of being able to publish on many?

These are just a few of the questions you should ask yourself when considering what road to take. Something notable that I want to stress is the importance of publishing the way that truly fits with your books, lifestyle, and choices.

If you know you're prone to writing short books, even if you're fast—wide is likely the better option. Consequently, if you write long but there's a gap between launches, KU would probably still benefit you, at least for a limited amount of time. It does no good to evaluate your books and publishing frequency if you don't make the logical choice that follows those questions.

This is true of many things in this book. I can only help you if you let me. The choice is yours, but hopefully this short review will help you decide which way you want your author career to go. You'll be one step closer to making six figures a year.

Start Ruling Your Author Empire Now

Subscribe to my newsletter to take the quiz on which way you should publish. If your answer is mixed, come back here and read up on the examples I give and what I'd recommend based on these factors.

Some Examples

I've discussed if your books are short or long. What does that mean?

If your books are under 45,000 words, I would call them short. Conversely, if they are over 80,000 words, I would call them long. Anything in between is simply average for this conversation. Let's say you fall within that average. What then?

Well, you need to look at the other factors. Are you publishing really frequently where you'd benefit from the rank boost? Frequent being more than four times a year. Or are you infrequent, with two releases a year or fewer? What if you say, "*Kel, I'm average here, too! I get out three or four books a year.*"

My response: Of course you do.

Because things can't ever be simple, am I right?

Let's talk risk

Does the idea of being at the mercy of Amazon cause you anxiety? If so, you've got your answer. Truth be told, this is the most important question.

Aurelia Jane, my coauthor, frequently tells me, "*If it costs you your peace, it's not worth it.*" It's stuck with me ever since.

If Amazon is the cost to your peace, IT'S NOT WORTH IT. I'm saying it in caps for the people in the back. Your peace of mind will directly affect your mindset, and you need to feel at ease with where you're publishing.

On the flip side of this, if uploading to multiple platforms, marketing multiple platforms, running ads to multiple platforms, and/or selling direct make your brain explode—**don't do it**.

Now, there's a difference between finding the prospect a little daunting because you don't know enough—and knowing enough but still finding it incredibly stressful. If you're the latter, you really should strongly consider staying in KU for your peace of mind. However, if you know how to run Facebook ads and it's just the time investment that makes you wary—do your research and think on it. Really evaluate what it is you're questioning and if you have a means of getting the answers.

Last but not least, let's talk about the most expensive resource there is.

You can't replenish it. You can never get a refund.

Time.

How to decide

Do you have the time to upload to multiple platforms? Do you have the time to run Facebook ads? Do you have time to promote freebies and apply to BookBubs and generally do all the things that go into being wide? I don't know, but you do.

If you're a single dad making do and writing in the evening when your kiddo is asleep, living the permanently exhausted pigeon life—odds are now isn't the right time to go wide. KU is simpler and less time-consuming in many ways. If you're the breadwinner mom who's out there killing it and needs this to pay what your day job does before going full time, it's probably worth a hard think. And if you write while the kids are at school and have a few extra hours every day, you're set, and this question of time probably isn't as pressing for you.

I can't make the choice for you

All I can do is ask that you really consider your life and circumstances when choosing which option is better for you. Remember, the choice isn't forever. You can always come back to it if things change. Lying to yourself for any reason won't help, so take off those glasses and make your decision. Then buckle in, because we're headed to the next part of *Rule Your Author Empire*: **Your Product**.

Start Ruling Your Author Empire Now

We've looked at all the ways you can publish, and the benefits and obstacles for each. Now it is time for you to decide which way you are going to publish. If you need some help, I offer a quiz that you can take when subscribing to my Rule Your Author Empire newsletter. Make a decision and stick with it. And if you choose to go hybrid or wide, don't be lackadaisical about your approach. Go get it. Conquer the hell out of it. After all, isn't that what great author empires do?

CHAPTER 5
BUILD THE FRAMEWORK OF YOUR AUTHOR EMPIRE

Let's talk about your product. For the next step in the *1 Year to 6 Figures* plan, I'm going to walk through the main factors that play a role in a reader picking up your book. Those factors are cover, blurb, reviews, and *maybe* the "Look inside." That's it. Those are the things a reader sees on a product page when they're deciding whether to give you a shot. So, we have to make sure your book gets a checkmark in every box.

YOUR COVER

We'll start with the cover because this is often the very first impression a reader has. Is your cover done by a professional that understands the genre? *Hint* — this means not done by you.

The importance of hiring a professional

Unless you are a professional cover designer (and even then), I often recommend working with someone else who does this for a living. Why? Because that thousand-yard view of your book is needed to make a simple but impactful cover. Authors often get tied up in the details. After all, the devil is in the details. But for covers, that's not the case.

Let's put this another way.

You want to make money, right? You put a price on your book, so clearly you do. That means the cover isn't for *you*. It's for your reader, and a cover designer that has made hundreds of other covers for your genre is your best chance of getting something beautiful that also hits the important notes of reader expectations.

Okay, Kel, you've sold me, but how do I FIND a great cover designer?

I have fabulous news for you. There is a place you can go on Facebook called the Cover Design Review Group. Authors post about the cover designers they do (and don't) recommend here. The best part? If you can't find someone that specializes in your genre, you can always post and ask the group. Odds are, we'll be able to scrounge up a few recommendations.

I've found several designers, but I don't know how to choose who's right for my project. Help!

This one is a little trickier. It's easy when you're faced with only one good option, but what do you do when there are several? Here are a few things you should look at to help make your decision.

1. Scheduling. How far out is the cover designer booking? One month? One year? More? This is super important because you have a timeline to adhere to for when you want this book release. If you're like me, who buys covers a year or more ahead of time, awesome. You have a lot of options then. If you wait till you have a finished draft? Well, that means you need someone yesterday.
2. Genres. Do they have covers that match your exact subgenre? Yes? Excellent. If the answer is no, I would pass on this designer.

3. Specialization. Do they specialize in the type of cover you want? Are they good at a person cover, object-based cover, or typography cover? Those are the three main types and oftentimes a designer is fabulous with one of them, but not all three. If they don't have examples of your desired cover type in their portfolio, I would pass on the designer for this project.

4. Testimonials. What do the authors who work with that designer have to say about them? Are they easy to work with? Do they make changes when requested or do they push back? Does this designer need "hand-holding?" I don't recommend choosing a designer who needs a lot of guidance for new authors because odds are, you don't understand the market well enough to do this.

5. Connection. Lastly, do you LOVE their covers? Do you look at their portfolio and think, "*Man, they'd be perfect for my book*?" It's okay if you don't have this, but if you've gone through all of the above questions and still have more than

one choice, then ask yourself whose style you prefer.

Genre Expectations

Ultimately, how do you know you're meeting genre expectations? There's one simple way to test this. Open up Amazon and go to your subgenre. Pull up the top twenty covers (especially if most of the top ten is one series). Put your cover up next to those and ask yourself, "Does my cover *fit* in with these covers?"

Notice I didn't say *blend* in. I said *fit*. That is an important distinction, because you'd like for yours to stand out a little bit if possible, but it has to be for the right reasons. Basically, because your cover is SO pretty or striking instead of because it looks homemade while the others do not.

An Example of What NOT to Do

This was my first cover. It's not a terrible cover, but even for the time period (2016) it wasn't great. The concept was there, but the execution wasn't. From the hard edges around the girls to the mixed Photoshop job blending, to the bright purple name at the bottom —there is A LOT that went wrong with this cover. My advice to you? Don't be this cover. Do your job as the author and find a good cover designer that understands the genre and how to craft a great cover in it that will help you—not hurt.

Important Takeaways

- Hire a good cover designer.
- Do your research.
- Ask for recommendations on who to use.
- Make sure your cover meets genre expectations.

YOUR BLURB

First things first: let's define blurb. You know that section on the product page that has a short, couple-sentence description about your book? That is the blurb. Now that everyone knows exactly what we're talking about, let's hit the highlights of what you need to do.

Is your blurb edited?

I mean really, is it completely free of errors? You've got fewer than two hundred words to use and convey to a reader the whole of your book, so they have to be perfect. This is so important because nothing turns off readers faster than an unedited blurb. For all they know, your book is full of mistakes too.

Does your blurb tell your reader what tropes are in your book?

We haven't discussed these in detail yet, but we will in the branding and marketing sections. For now, let's assume your book has *some* tropes. Those need to be front and center so your reader knows what to expect, and I don't mean listing them out. Let me show you what I mean.

Case Study: *Reject Me*

This is the blurb for my bestselling book, *Reject Me*:

"Markus Del Reyes, I reject you."
He left me no choice.
I refuse to spend the rest of my life with my childhood bully for a mate. I may be a cursed shifter, incapable of shifting—but I wasn't desperate.
Not till the Alpha Supreme cast me out of the House of Fire and Fluorite for rejecting his son.
Now I'm packless.
Homeless.
No longer under the protection of a House.
Until the dark vampire king of Blood and Beryl turns his sights on me.
In return for protection from my former House.
I have to become his fake mate.
I'll be a queen and a fraud.
It's a treacherous lie to live—and I find myself forgetting what's real and what's not with every stolen touch and heated kiss we share.
What starts as a business arrangement turns complicated when my heat hits, and the king insists on being the one to help me through it.
I've lost everything for doing what I know is right, but the greatest danger I ever faced was never losing my life ... it was opening my cursed heart.

Right from the get-go we have, "**Markus Del Reyes, I reject you.**" This screams: rejected mate and shifter romance. Boom. Two for one, folks.

Next, we have, "**I refuse to spend the rest of my life with my childhood bully for a**

mate." This tells the reader that our heroine comes from a troubled past.

The next line, "**I may be a cursed shifter, incapable of shifting—but I wasn't desperate**" tells the reader she's an underdog—a self-assured one, but still an underdog.

"**Not till the Alpha Supreme cast me out of the House of Fire and Fluorite for rejecting his son. Now I'm** *packless*. *Homeless*. **No longer under the protection of a House.**" This part is my inciting incident. The thing that triggers the beginning of the story.

The next line has "dark vampire king." This tells the reader several things. First, that they can expect a darker hero. Second, he's a vampire and therefore at odds to some degree with our heroine because she's a shifter. Third, he's a king. Royalty, baby; it's a trope.

"**In return for protection from my former House, I have to become his** *fake mate*." This says that they make a deal *and* that there is fake dating, a trope that was HUGE at the time this was releasing.

The section, "**I'll be a queen and a fraud. It's a treacherous lie to live—and I find myself forgetting what's real and what's not**

with every stolen touch and heated kiss we share," reinforces the fake-dating trope and pushes the romance aspect. Readers should know this will probably be spicy with phrases like "stolen touch" and "heated kiss."

Next it reads, "**What starts as a business arrangement turns complicated when my heat hits, and the king insists on being the one to help me through it.**" The concept of shifters going into heat is another trope. This also backs up the spice level, because no closed-door romance is going to have shifter heats. At least, not one I've ever read.

And last but not least, we finish with, "**I've lost everything for doing what I know is right, but the greatest danger I ever faced was never losing my life … it was opening my cursed heart.**" Not only is she an underdog, but this heroine has a heart of gold. In all subgenres of romance, readers like to imagine themselves as the heroine. That means, oftentimes, that the heroine needs to be likable. I made sure to convey that in my blurb, along with the "dark and mysterious" hero who's only got eyes for her.

This blurb is chock-full of tropes, so it's really no wonder that this book has made six figures by itself. That's right. This one title made over $100,000 dollars. That's the beauty of positioning your book properly.

Important Takeaways

- Make sure your blurb is edited.
- Utilize all the relevant tropes in your story.
- Keep it under two hundred words.

REVIEWS

You're probably wondering why "Reviews" is listed here when you can't control your reviews. That is true, to a certain extent. While you can't control who reviews or what star rating they leave, you can *influence* them.

*"But Kel, *gasp*, what do you mean?"*

Early Reviews

I'm talking about ARC (Advance Reader Copy) readers. Early reviewers. People who win a copy of the book before launch. All of these readers are potential reviewers, and by cultivating who gets access to your book first, you get to decide the initial impression your book makes on launch, before organic readers can impact it.

To find these early reviewers you can reach out to your existing audience if you have one and get people to sign up via a Google form or by joining a Facebook group. You can also reach out to reviewers and ask if they'd be interested in reading a copy of your book. Lastly, you can always put a broad call out into the ether that is social media and see if you get some bites. You may or may not do this one, depending on what you write, since the wrong reviewers can also have a negative impact on launch if you get too many of them.

By "wrong reviewers" I mean readers that aren't readers of your genre. For instance, a hardcore military sci-fi reader would not likely be interested in, and would certainly not be a good fit for, a romantasy. By making sure your cover and blurb show clear genre expectations, you can find the right readers for *you*.

To distribute your ARCs, I recommend you use BookFunnel or Booksprout. I'm sure there are other similar services around but those are the main two I know of that require very little effort.

The ONLY Road

Another thing that's important to note about

reviews is that you should never respond to them. Nothing looks worse than an angry author coming after someone who left a one-star review, no matter the reason. Yep, so whatever case you're thinking of right now that makes you want to go, *"But Kel!"* Nope. It still counts. Don't respond. Take the high road.

Why Critical Reviews Matter

If your rating is on the lower end and you've got a significant number of reviews (several hundred minimum), it's important to look at *why* they are low. Is there something that a large number of people are repeatedly saying? Is your opening too slow? Is your main character too unlikable? I use these examples, because that was the feedback I received on my first book. Mind you, that book has thousands of reviews and a 4.4 star rating average, which isn't bad. Probably 10% of my reviews mention one or both of these things though. That's a lot of readers, and those are just the ones that left a review. How many tried the book, but couldn't get into it so they just DNF'd (did not finish) it? Sometimes it hurts to hear, but criticism can be a good thing. How else will we know what to improve as authors?

It's important to note that negative reviews can

also help your book find the right readers. Let's take a steamy romance book that has the cover, title, and blurb all perfectly branded. If this book got a one star saying it's too much sex, well that's free promotion basically. I can't count the number of readers (including myself) that picked up a book because a negative review hated something that they loved.

Important Takeaways

- Take advantage of being your own publisher and generate early buzz with reviews.
- Never respond to poor reviews, the only person that will look bad is you.
- Don't avoid reviews entirely. Read the negative ones to see what you can learn from them.
- Remember that negative reviews can also help you sometimes.

YOUR "LOOK INSIDE," I.E. YOUR FIRST CHAPTER

The last thing that some readers will look at when deciding whether to buy your book or not is your

"Look Inside." This is your very first chapter and a bit more, since Amazon and several other retailers show approximately 5% of the book as a sample.

Hook, Line, and Sinker

When readers look at this, they are likely looking for several things. The first and most important is: Does your chapter grab them? Do you drone on with inner monologue for most of it and complete it with a description of the hero or heroine looking in the mirror at themselves? (I do not recommend this.) Or is it fast paced? Is there some sort of tension, whether it be from action or intrigue?

While many readers don't download a sample before buying, rest assured that your opening chapter is arguably your most important because if you're going to gain or lose a reader, odds are it will be there. Make sure to hook them in those first five to ten pages, or you'll likely see it reflected in poor sales, less than stellar read-throughs, and returns.

Perfecting the Vision

Like your blurb, you'll want to make sure that your book is edited. This isn't a craft book, so I won't go into it much, but here's a quick breakdown of the kinds of editing there is.

- **Developmental edits**. This is a high-level edit that looks at your *story* and the characters' journey. Developmental edits also address plot holes and often include notes in tracked changes, along with a several-page breakdown of your book and what could be improved on story-wise. This does not get into word choices or sentence structure, only the story itself.

- **Line edits**. A line editor works sentence by sentence on the *structure* of your writing. Are you telling the story in the most effective way possible, while keeping in line with your voice? Sentences are restructured in this kind of edit.

- **Copy edits**. Copyediting focuses on the mechanics. This looks like missing commas, double words, correcting punctuation, etc. Copyeditors are making sure your manuscript follows a style guide, often the Chicago Manual of Style.

- **Proofreading**. At this stage, they are looking for typos. That's it.

First-Time Authors

I cannot stress enough the importance of editing. It doesn't matter how good your cover, blurb, and first chapter are if the rest of the book can't follow up. Some of the places you can find editors are Reedsy and asking in author Facebook groups for recommendations.

But remember, we live in the internet age. Anyone can claim to be an editor. It's important for you to do your research when selecting someone and to get a sample edit. Ideally, you'd get sample edits from several editors, so you have something to compare. It's true that we don't see our own flaws, which can make selecting a good editor difficult, but you can see clear as day if one editor missed things that another picked up on in a sample. I highly recommend doing this.

The Cost of an Editor

I'm not going to pretend here, editing is expensive. For a 40,000 word+ manuscript you should expect to pay at least a grand if not more.

"Gasp! But Kel, I can't afford that!"

Listen, I know it's a lot. Believe me, I get it. When I published my first book, I had to save up tips for seven months working at a crappy pizza place that didn't value me just to be able to afford to publish. Maybe find a side hustle in the meantime to help you bring in some extra cash that you can store away. Publishing is expensive, but in an ideal situation, you'll make all your money back plus profit.

If you truly cannot find the money for an editor no matter what, my suggestion is to compile a group of people willing to alpha read and point things out. I don't like this approach because it's hard enough to find one qualified person, let alone several willing to do it for free. Normal people don't know what to keep and what to change, and this isn't their fault. Oftentimes it's because they can't separate their wants as a reader versus what's needed for the book to work. For these reasons, I would only do this if you have *literally* no other option.

Important Takeaways

- Make sure your manuscript is edited. DO NOT SKIP THIS STEP. It's super important to produce a professional product!

- Ensure your first chapter has a strong hook and incentivizes readers to keep reading.

YOUR PRODUCT

This concludes the section on Building the Framework to Your Author Empire. If you've been doing this for a while, this might not be new information, but it's a good reminder that at the end of the day, these are the most important pieces you're building with. No matter how good the marketing is, nothing can save a bad product, so make sure to invest the time needed into making yours great. In doing so, you'll actually work less to sell said product.

My bestselling book is one that I've put the least amount of marketing into. I ran a Goodreads giveaway, shared with my newsletter and social media, and ran a $20-per-day Facebook ad for a couple months. By all means, this book should have had a mediocre release, but guess what? It sat in the top 500 on Amazon for six months.

That is the power of having a killer book that is packaged the *right* way.

Start Ruling Your Author Empire Now

Review the following checklist for your next launch or complete the sections labeled "Building the Framework" in the **workbook** (this is a free download you get for joining my newsletter at RuleYour AuthorEmpire.com). Is everything checked off? Make sure each item is completed before launch, so you can give your book the best chance of succeeding.

- Is your cover professionally designed?
- Does your cover meet genre expectations?
- Is the blurb edited?
- Does the blurb tell the reader what tropes are in your book?
- Is the book edited?
- Are you sending out ARCs or some form of advance copies to readers that will hopefully review?

CHAPTER 6
DECKING OUT YOUR AUTHOR EMPIRE

BRANDING

This chapter is all about branding, which encompasses your books, your name typography on them, your logo, the tropes you use, your covers, your genre—if it's something you are putting out into the world, it's part of your branding.

This is important to understand because...

YOU ARE DEFINED BY YOUR BRAND.

For instance, if you primarily write paranormal romance novels, you would be considered a paranormal romance author. Similarly, if you often have covers that feature a single girl and a wolf, those sorts of covers would become your brand. This isn't a bad thing, in fact, it's very good. Homing in on your brand is so incredibly important because this is what you will be known for. Which means your core readership that loves those things will continue to grow, and always pick up your next book as long as it falls inside your brand. This is a huge component of the *1 Year to 6 Figures* plan.

WHAT DO I MEAN BY THIS?

Let's say you write shifter books, but then decide to put out an angel romance. It might do fine, but you'll most likely see a drop in core readership because you delivered something unexpected. If your readers are used to reading shifter books and you deliver something new, not all of them will be interested in that new thing. However, if you continue to deliver shifter books, your core readership that loves that will grow over time. It will become a rising tide that will carry you in rank if you're in KU, or if you're wide, eventually to bestseller lists.

Now, if you're thinking, *"But Kel, I've already*

written x number of novels and they're all in different subgenres," girl (or guy), let me tell you. **Me too.**

That's why this one is such a huge deal, and it was a mistake I made again and again.

I've got books in high fantasy, why choose paranormal romance, young adult. Really, they're all over the place. All my books are fantasy, but they're largely different sub-genres in fantasy. At a certain point, my career stagnated because of this. But guess what? It doesn't have to stay that way.

Look at what has made the most money and keep writing that going forward. Just because we made mistakes early in our career doesn't mean they have to define us. What's important is learning from those things and then pivoting to try to improve our branding with time. And it will take time.

LOOKING AT MY BRAND

With how many genres I wrote in and the types of creatures I used, I didn't realize this lesson until the last year or so. Now that I have, I'm curving my branding to keep writing the same genres that my readers keep showing up for and love. Unfortunately, my sphere is a bit bigger than I'd like because I have several very distinct audiences with KU and wide, plus MF (Male/Female romance), and reverse harem/why choose romance. Due to this vast difference between genres and audiences, I sat down and evaluated my brand, what it's currently known for, and *what I want it to be known for.* This is what I came up with:

While I have a large reverse harem audience, I also have a significant MF audience. While reverse harem readers will often read MF, the same is not true in reverse. Therefore, to not limit myself, I'm going to continue writing primarily MF romance.

95% of my catalog is wide. I'm what is often referred to as hybrid.

Hybrid can mean someone who has books that are both traditionally published and Indie published, but for how I am going to reference it, hybrid means some of my books are wide and some are in Kindle Unlimited.

Kindle Unlimited (Forever?)

The three books in Kindle Unlimited are my newest releases in the last two years. They also are books with a *heavy* KU audience. This means over 80% of the money these books make is from page reads in KU. It's not surprising, given they are long books. And even after a year or more has passed, they're still ranking fairly high. This is why I left them in Kindle Unlimited for the time being.

Wide (for the Win!)

The rest of my catalog is wide. Being wide allows me to sell directly to readers through my own online store, which is how I make **60–70%** of my income. Amazon makes up about **20–30%** and the wide platforms take the remaining **10% (or less)**. It changes every month, depending on what advertisements I'm running and if I had a BookBub Featured Deal. We'll talk more on this in the next chapter.

KU to Wide

Due to these factors, I decided to release into KU after having a wide preorder first. This means I put up the book for sale *everywhere* first, then after it releases, I take it down from all places *outside* Amazon. Once it's down from all retailers, I put my book in Kindle Unlimited. When the book rank drops enough, and it's no longer getting the perks of being in KU, I move it back wide.

This works for me. It may not work for you, and it's certainly not conventional. It's a bit more work as well, but part of building a core readership is making sure they feel valued. If I only catered to wide or KU, I'd be alienating part of my readership when it comes to new releases. I don't want to do that, and I have the time to invest in both, so I took a path that lets me cater to both.

With branding, the more specific you can be, the better off you are. I transitioned with my brand for several years. That might seem like a long time, but it was necessary to not confuse my readership or risk my income taking a dive.

TIME TO TALK ABOUT THE "T" WORD

There's another way branding takes form and it's a pretty big one that I haven't touched on yet: tropes.

Or perhaps, more accurately, the *what* and the *why* of tropes.

Tropes are common scenarios that take place in your book that readers LOVE. Some examples of them are:

- Enemies-to-lovers
- Secret baby
- Instalove
- Rejected mates

These are just a few, and far from the only ones.

For a much more comprehensive list, you should check out the *Trope Thesaurus* by Jennifer Hilt. She has pretty much every trope you can think of in there, along with a great explanation for each. "The Trope Song" by Lisa Daily is also a fantastic (and short) way to check out some of the bigger ones.

Think about what tropes you automatically gravitate toward in your writing. Do you just love a good friends-to-lovers romance? What about only one bed? These are part of your branding, but they're not the only factor in the recipe of what makes a book tasty to readers.

Like a chef knows the value of using butter to make a recipe tasty, be deliberate in your choices as an author, and create a tasty experience your readers will remember—and want more of—over and over again.

I'm going to borrow a passage from T. Taylor's *Universal Fantasy List: Romance*.

Trope: The familiar thing your romance is.

Universal Fantasy (UF): What makes that trope taste good.

Take the trope **Beauty and the Beast,** for example. This trope is delicious because it has Universal Fantasies like **Beast Healed/Tamed by Love** being played out through the story. Examples that show this trope are *Beastly* (film), *Once Upon a Time* (TV show), and *A Ruin of Roses* (spicy romance book).

Think of it this way: tropes are the *what* of your story, while "butter" is the *why*.

Both tropes and Universal Fantasies are tasty and delicious to your readers. Don't shy away from them. You're running a business here and just like any good restaurant chef, you know the value of butter. *Am I right?* Of course I am!

For more information on this concept, you should also totally read T. Taylor's book, *7 Figure Fiction*, if you haven't yet.

Back to the "T" word. Now, some people say, *"But I don't write tropes."* Let me tell you something: **no idea is completely original or unique**. The inspiration came from somewhere, so if you hate on tropes and Universal Fantasies, you're holding yourself back from a writing career that could flourish.

Tropes are gold. Or more realistically, they're a huge asset that helps bring in the money. Using the same ones again and again is actually a good thing. If your readers liked it once, odds are they will again, with a slightly different spin on it.

What's more, readers these days are sophisticated. Platforms like TikTok and Instagram have conditioned readers to talk in tropes. They know and discuss the ones they love and respond well to marketing that highlights them. This is because tropes help readers find more stories they're already predisposed to like.

THE DEVIL IS IN THE DETAILS

Something I've come to realize over the years is that it's not what you write, it's *how* you write it that really matters. Readers read for the journey, and the end is just an excuse to begin. **So, think about ways that you can mix up the journey while keeping the core beats of your bestselling stuff the same.**

I don't make many guarantees, because I can't promise things will work for you as they have for me and many other authors I've worked with, but this is one of them: *You are guaranteed to grow your core reader base if you stick to these principles and refine your branding.*

Branding is just a way of communicating the type of books you write to your readers and potential readers. Just like you know what to expect every time you walk into an Apple store or Taco Bell, your branding should tell readers exactly what they need to know to figure out if you write the kinds of books they like. Consider if someone were to describe your books to a friend. **The things they'd say about them, my dear reader, is your branding**.

SOCIAL MEDIA

The last type of branding I want to touch on is perhaps one of the most important forms in the *1 Year to 6 Figures* plan, and that's your social media. Here is a list of some of the ways social media and branding intersect.

- How your name is stylized on your covers and in your graphics, as in the typeface or font you use.
- The colors on your covers and teasers
- The tone of voice in your posts or "vibes" that you're putting out
- The images you use for teasers and other author-specific posts

These all make up **your branding** and they are key to creating a harmonious look at *you*, the bestselling author.

Your Typeface

Let's take a deeper dive into typeface, otherwise known as font. What font you use is incredibly important. You may even choose to use multiple fonts. You'll want to take care that whatever you select is readable on a range of images and posts, without readers needing to zoom in. You may love a super-unique font and want to use it, but if readers can't read your posts, they don't have a positive impact. In fact, it could have a negative impact because they start to associate those unreadable fonts *with* you.

Trademarking Your Name

Something to consider with typeface is trademarking your author name in the branding fonts you use, and I'm not talking Times New Roman. If you have a specific font you always use for your name on your social media and book covers, it's not a bad idea to get that trademarked. While you can't "own" a name, you can own your branding. It can be better safe than sorry, especially in the case of someone else stumbling upon your pen name and deciding to use it to publish books themselves.

Your Social Media Handles

Speaking of author names, your social media

handles are also part of your branding. For my Instagram, I am @authorkelcarpenter and on TikTok I'm @kelcarpenterauthor. This discrepancy isn't something I'm thrilled by, but I've got it in enough books at this point, it would be a bit of a pain to change. That said, if you're starting out, you can avoid that issue by making sure what social media profiles you have are always consistent. Furthermore, I actually recommend '@pennameauthor' over '@authorpenname' because there are A LOT of @Author(insert name) when typing it into the search bar, whereas your name is specific to you.

Your Social Media Images

Images are tricky, particularly book teaser images. If there's too much going on in them, it will be hard to read any type that's on top of the image. Your eye doesn't know where to look because is *everywhere.* To avoid this, it's easiest if you use images that are largely dark so that light font shows up, or vice versa. You will also need to take into account the length of your teaser, not just the font used or image choice. Longer teasers need very simple images because the words will need to be smaller. Choosing the wrong image can oftentimes make the graphic look "homemade," which is the last thing you want. A successful author career is built on clear branding.

Burnout

Another piece of advice I wish I could have given myself when I started is: don't overdo it.

The faster you burn yourself out, the harder your author empire will be to rule.

What do I mean by overdoing it? Don't join every social media platform with the purpose of creating content daily. Odds are, you'll burn yourself out. Instead, pick one to two that you vibe with, and perhaps already use, to be your main social media author accounts. In my case, I enjoy Instagram, cross-post with TikTok, and call it good.

What do you see when you evaluate your branding with a critical eye? Be honest now, because rose-colored glasses won't be worn by potential readers.

SOME EXAMPLES

Do you keep your life to yourself or post about it broadly? Both are okay, but I might encourage you to be mindful of what you post because the internet is forever. If readers see your post hating on one-star reviews, for example, that's not the best look. Neither is complaining about

Goodreads, or venting about that fight with your mom.

My best friend and I have a joke. It's a Squidward meme that says, "We post memes here, sir" and anytime we see some craziness going on in authorlandia, we send this to one another. Why? Because we're not going to touch it with a ten-foot pole—as authors and as readers.

Where's the line?

That's not to say never talk about your life; if you're a sharer, then share away. But make it relevant and positive overall. One author I follow shared her journey exploring more *ahem* adventurous bedroom activities with her newsletter and it was incredibly engaging, especially since she writes on the spicier side of life in her books. It was appropriate for the readership.

Another author I adore to pieces writes romcoms and regularly shares her #fails that are hilarious. This is a way to utilize parts of your life to make your brand more personable, and let me tell you, readers eat that stuff up. In the information era, people want to know the authors they are reading are just like them. That we're human beings who laugh, and strive, and grow, just like them. That idea is often muddied for authors who struggle to draw the line with how much, or how little, to share.

That's not to say that you *have* to share. My coauthor, Aurelia Jane, for example, is incredibly private. She doesn't have her face as her profile picture. She doesn't post pictures of her kids. She rarely, if ever, talks about them online. This is who she is. So, what does she post instead? Well, memes, duh. Also, hilarious text conversations she and I have. Notes we leave each other on manuscripts. Pictures of her asshole cats taking up her lap and preventing work. These are things our readers love because it's a little look inside to who Aurelia is without giving away information she is uncomfortable with. That's your main goal here.

COAUTHOR BRANDING

Coauthoring is something I get asked about **a lot**, probably because half my catalog is cowritten. In this section, I'm going to review branding specifically, and how that works with cowriting.

Spoiler alert: it's still super important!

Important Factors to Consider When Choosing a Partner

When taking on a coauthor, you need to

consider their branding. Is it similar to yours? Do you share a readership? This is important because if your branding is too different from each other's, you will inevitably stray from *someone's* branding, whether it's yours or your partner's. Oftentimes, writers say to branch out, and pick someone with different audiences than yours. This isn't exactly a good thing. It muddies your core audience and confuses your branding.

Instead, I recommend picking someone that's right alongside you in the charts and writes the same kind of things as you. Then you can double down on that core readership! Alternatively, you can do what I've done with my main coauthor, Aurelia Jane, where Aurelia launched her pen name with our first cowrite, *Dark Horse*. When writing it, we catered to my existing brand but also kept in mind what Aurelia and I envisioned for our **joint brand**. This worked quite well in our case and my core audience responded positively.

An Example of Coauthor Branding

Now that we've addressed *how* to pick someone, or at least what to consider when thinking with branding in mind, let's look at coauthor branding. What does your brand look like *together?* For this, I'm going to use myself and Aurelia Jane as an example (again).

We made a choice when we wrote our first book together to get coauthor branding done. This means we had our names stylized for how they will appear on *every* cover. It's different from my individual branding because it teaches readers what to expect when they see both of us versus just me.

For instance, Aurelia is hilarious and dives much deeper into the feels than I do. She writes long conversations that pull the reader in. This is different from just Kel, who tends to write content that is pithy, or to the point, in other words. Our coauthor branding communicates that to readers— they know what to expect when they pick up a Kel Carpenter and Aurelia Jane book. It's about the use of our names and the kind of stories we write. There will be laughs and maybe a tear or two shed. There will potentially be a hilarious sidekick. There are always themes of found family and positive female relationships, as well as diversity in the color and ethnicity of our characters.

This, you guys, is branding at its core. Teaching

readers what to expect from *you* (and your coauthor).

Start Ruling Your Author Empire Now

I challenge you to evaluate your brand.

Sit down and list every book you've written. Look at how much each has made. Look at the read through on series. Read through is the percentage of readers that read from book one to book two, from book two to book three, and so on. Next, pick your bestselling story that hopefully you enjoyed writing, and figure out how to do another like it. Use the same tropes, use similar colors on your cover and graphics. Follow the same beats. Recreate your bestseller by following the path you already set, but make it even *better*.

Now, if you're looking over your books and say, *"Kel, I don't have anything that's worthy of recreating. I need your help to figure out where to go next."* We can do that, too.

If you're wanting to go toward something new, I suggest a multistep process that the author community likes to call "write to market." Instead of just telling you that, though, I'm going to break it down for you, too.

WHERE THE LAND MEETS THE SEA

"Write to market" means looking at what audiences exist in the market and then writing a book or series for this voracious audience. It doesn't mean writing something you hate. Nor does it make you sell out. It means you want to make money doing what you love and find more readers. If that's you, you're in luck. I'll explain how you do it.

You evaluate Amazon and look at a genre you're interested in. I'm going to use paranormal romance as an example because it's what I'm most familiar with. On Amazon, paranormal romance is a category. It shows you the top hundred books in it. Take those hundred books and jot them down. Write out what tropes they have, what creatures they use, and what their covers look like. Then evaluate the similarities.

A conclusion you may come to is that they share dragon shifter romance with rejected mates and trials (this is just an example). So you would sit down and plot, or begin writing if you're a pantser, a book that at its core would be a dragon shifter romance with the rejected mate trope and trials. It's really that easy and doable. I promise.

Start Ruling Your Author Empire Now

If you don't have a bestseller that you'd like to emulate going forward, do the research for a "write to market" project.

1. Pick a genre.
2. Go to Amazon and research that genre.
3. Decide what tropes you think you could write into your chosen story idea.
4. Plot it, or skip this step.
5. Write it!

That's it. That is how you craft a bestseller. If you need a second opinion or still feel shaky on your understanding, look at what courses I am offering for a more in-depth take on some of these topics. I like to do office hours, which gives students the opportunity to get personalized feedback.

CHAPTER 7
PAVING THE ROADS TO YOUR AUTHOR EMPIRE

This section is titled "Paving the Roads to Your Author Empire" because roads are how you get from place to place, and in this section, we're going to cover how you lead readers straight into the heart of your author empire, i.e. your books. Whether you're traditionally published or self-published, there should be little gold nuggets of information for everyone in this chapter that will bring you one step closer to finishing the *1 Year to 6 Figures* plan.

MARKETING

This almost feels like too big a term to summarize, but I'm going to try my best here. Marketing, in short, is the activity of promoting or selling your products or services. Sounds simple when I put it that way, right? That's because it is, but do you remember that analogy I used before? About how it's hard to see the forest through the trees? This is *especially* true for authors when it comes to marketing. While writing is second nature to the vast majority of us, going out of our way to try to sell someone on our book? Not so much.

The reality is that marketing is a huge part of our job, whether we're self-published or traditionally published. It's so big, in fact, that I'd say I spend a third of my working hours just doing admin related to marketing. If you're thinking, *"Wow, Kel, but I want to write full time not market full time,"* I have bad news for you. Writing is only 30-40% of my job as a full-time author. Yep. I said it. Editing is another 30% and marketing is pretty much the rest.

So, with that in mind, let's break it down further.

There are two types of marketing out there. There's passive marketing and active marketing. What does this mean?

- **Passive marketing** is marketing that you set up once and it continues to work without any additional effort on your part. This happens when a reader reads your book and then goes on to read your whole catalog because you sold them on your writing with book one. Another example of passive marketing is when you put a sign-up for your newsletter in the back matter of your book and gain subscribers that way. There are lots and lots of ways to passively market and we're going to touch on a lot of them.

- **Active marketing** requires you to put in the effort. You're going out of your way to reach new readers for a specific promotion. Some examples of this include newsletter swaps, promotion sites like BookBub, and reader giveaways.

Important Takeaways

- Marketing is a huge part of being an author, whether you're indie or traditionally published.
- Passive marking is a set-it-and-forget-it method. You put in the work once and continue to benefit for months or years.

- Active marketing is more intentional and usually involves working with other authors or promotion sites.

PASSIVE MARKETING

Passive Marketing is vital to the *1 Year to 6 Figures* plan. After all, you can't be everywhere at once. That doesn't mean your marketing can't be. By anticipating where customers will be, you can set up to passively market your books with these methods. In doing this, you're working smarter—not harder —and saving valuable time for the things that matter.

Newsletters

This is a huge way to break down the barrier between you and your readers. Newsletters are incredibly effective because they cut everyone else out of the equation and lets you communicate directly with your readers.

I want to stress the importance of not simply relying on social media, because those platforms aren't reliable. The algorithm could change. Your account could get shut down. I can't tell you how many people have told me they went viral on TikTok but then something happened that they could not control and now they can't get any traction. At the end of the day, you don't want to be at the mercy of another platform when it comes to talking to your readers, and newsletters are arguably the best way to avoid that happening.

It's also worth noting that **it is five to seven times more expensive to acquire a new customer than it is to keep your existing ones**. If you can build a successful and engaging newsletter, you may be able to circumvent social media altogether for the most part. Wouldn't that be nice?

First-Timers

The newsletter services I think are best for first-time authors are MailerLite and Flodesk. MailerLite has a free plan for up to 1,000 subscribers (at the time of writing this) and Flodesk is a flat fee of $35/month that doesn't go up no matter how many subscribers you have. My advice to those starting out would be to start with MailerLite to minimize costs and move to Flodesk once your list gets bigger. You can even keep MailerLite for its integration capabilities and export your subscribers over to Flodesk every month to keep the costs down and harness the best of both platforms.

Grow Your List

As for how you can grow your list, that's where the passive marketing comes into play. You can put a link to your newsletter in the back of your book. An example of this looks like:

Join Kel's Newsletter: www.kelcarpenter.com

This is you, anticipating readers will get to the end of the book and are therefore primed and ready to follow you, which is true! Gaining followers this way is the cheapest and one of the most effective strategies around.

Another quick and easy way to grow your newsletter is to write a bonus chapter or epilogue and have readers subscribe to your newsletter to read it. This is one that I used in my most recent release:

Thank you for reading MATE ME! We hope you enjoyed Reagan and Caius' love story. To read a special, extended epilogue of Reagan and Caius, join our newsletter HERE.

I've done both and seen steady, reliable results.

On another note, I am NOT a big believer in newsletter builders because I think they...

1. Are mostly freebie seekers.

2. Junk up your email.

3. Lower your open rates.

Instead, I think it's better to let your newsletter organically build on its own, from people that find you online or through your books. If they loved one book, it's an easier sell to get them to read another.

Newsletter Autoresponder

Creating a funnel for new sign-ups is a great way to maintain a healthy newsletter when onboarding new subscribers, while also weeding out those that might only be interested in a free book.

"But Kel, what is a funnel?"

Great question!

A funnel is a series of emails that go out over time in order to achieve a goal. Obviously, our main goal is to get them to buy more books, but if you just hit them with "Buy this book!" emails, I hate to break it to you, but they're going to unsubscribe, like, yesterday.

To sell books, you need to build some reader loyalty. Ways you can do this include sending out emails to increase engagement rates by asking a question, increasing open rates by offering a free book, or helping the reader become more familiar with you and your work through a more personalized approach that doesn't ask them directly to buy your book.

You can also set up funnels for reader magnets specifically if you want to take a more in-depth approach. By this, I mean if you have a reader magnet, you can create a funnel specifically for that offer and see how it converts with readers over time, compared to your general funnel. This sort of funnel might be related to a specific book or series instead of all your books, so it's going to look a little different in that you might focus on specific scenes or characters instead of a different series every email, as you might in a general welcome funnel.

Social Media

Similar to newsletters, you can put links to your social media in the back of your books so that readers know where they can follow you. Then every time you post, you're reaching all those readers that single action gained for you. You can double down on this by using apps like This, Then, That or repurpose.io, which cross-posts for you.

ALSO BY THE AUTHOR

This is a section you can add pretty easily in the back of your books if you use a program like

Vellum to format. Even if you don't, it's still very doable. "Also by" sections are essentially just a place to list out your other books with links for where to buy them. You've already done all the work by having them read one of your books. If they loved it and want to try more, providing them a place to browse is a must.

To learn more about back matter and what's important to have there, I recommend Skye Warren's method that she talks about in *The Bestselling Author Next Door*. This book was highly instrumental in shaping how I view creating an author empire, and back matter is just one of the very important things that Skye talks about. The short explanation of it, is she recommends you have:

- The cover
- A short intro
- A sneak peek to the next book you want your readers to buy

It's a very simple but effective method. I've implemented it on all my own works.

SMS Setup

This kind of marketing is the new kid on the

block in terms of ways to contact readers. The way it works is you have a text line set up that readers can send a single word or phrase to, and that puts them on your texting/SMS list. It's very easy to set up and much like a newsletter or social media, all you have to do is put it in the back of a book for you to start getting sign-ups. Then, whenever you have a sale or new release, you can rattle off a text to the list. Easy-peasy! The greatest upside of this method is that because it's new, readers aren't as inundated with messages from other authors yet, unlike email.

Some SMS service providers to check out are . . .

- Textedly
- Klaviyo
- Twilio
- SimpleTexting
- EZ Texting

Book Lists/ Reading Order

Creating a list of all the books you've written with the reading order is a great way to simplify the buying process for readers. Bonus points if you include links for where to buy every book. This is a simple thing to do that you can update with new releases and upload to your website.

Another place you can utilize reading lists is at author events. Authors Deanna Roy and Vanessa Vale both talk about having a printed book list for signings. Readers are primed and ready when they come to your table. What better way to market to them than to have all your books neatly laid out on paper that they can take with them to look up later? What's more, you can add a QR code with a link-tr.ee for where to grab the newest releases and follow you on social media or your newsletter.

Important Takeaways

- Part of working less means utilizing every tool you have available, and that includes your books. Make sure your back matter includes a link to your newsletter, social media, SMS text line, and has an "Also by the Author" section.
- To keep a newsletter healthy and engaged, it's a good idea to build out an effective autoresponder funnel that lets them get to know you and your books.

- Lastly, having a book list available on your website is a good way to help readers support you. Make their job easy! And don't forget to bring a hard copy of it to any signings you attend.

ACTIVE MARKETING

This kind of marketing involves your business interacting with another entity to gain new readership. These promotions tend to be more effective but have an expiration date. In other words, this marketing is very deliberate.

Newsletter swaps

You agree to share another author's book in return for them sharing yours in their newsletter. Usually, authors only do this for a sale or a new release to drive more buzz toward it. It can be a great way to find new readers if you know the author you are swapping with has a similar brand to yours. If you're going to swap though, make sure the expectations are clear, i.e., if it's a solo swap, one of two or three recommendations, if the blurb will be included, etc.

A note of caution in swapping: Don't load up your newsletter with 10+ recommendations and call it good. For one, you'll get a bad reputation with other authors. Secondly, you should try to have a purpose behind every newsletter that isn't swapping, whether that's promoting a sale or new release, a bonus scene, a teaser, a cover reveal, or something else—the point is there should be some kind of purpose to it.

Promotion sites

Promotion sites are places where you pay a fee in exchange for them promoting your book to their readers, often at a discounted price. BookBub is the most well-known example of this, but they're far from the only one. Some other examples include:

- Bargain Booksy
- Book Barbarian
- Book Cave
- Fussy Librarian

Paid promotion sites aren't the only option. BookFunnel also has a server for those hosting promotions to list them and have other authors sign up. Most of them are free to join and have minimal share requirements. You might not get as many downloads or readers from them, but it's a great way to grow if you're tight on funds.

Paid Newsletters

Similar to promotion sites, you pay to be featured in a newsletter, but don't have to feature anything in return. This can be a great option if you don't have a lot of author contacts that write in your genre or to reach additional readers beyond your circle.

Reader Giveaways

These can look like a number of things. One common setup is you and a set number of authors in your genre team up and offer a reader giveaway. To enter the giveaway readers will have to like the post, comment on it, and follow all the authors involved. The idea behind this is to attract them as a potential reader to your social media so that you can sell to them again and again when you have a new release.

Another option to do giveaway-based promotions is through Goodreads. For $119 you can promote your book on their site for a giveaway and readers have to click Want to Read in order to join. What's more, on release day, all those readers get a notification that this book they wanted to read is now available! This is one of my favorite ways to create early buzz for a release.

Influencers and Book Boxes

Book boxes can be a fantastic way to create organic buzz and can be customized to be as exclusive as you'd like. They can be offered to only Bookstagrammers and BookTokers, or to the broader reader public. You can charge for them if you're looking to promote mainly to mega fans and smaller accounts or send for free if you're trying to reach the broader public through exposure. You have complete control over what goes in them. The options are limitless.

Case Study: *Mate Me*

Recently, I put together a book box for an upcoming release. I started by deciding what the max amount per box was that I wanted to spend, which was $25 USD. From there, I picked out items and got quotes from different swag providers. Once I locked in what I was offering, I created a Google form for book influencers and posted it on social media. I ran a very low-spend ad for $5 a day to get it in front of as many readers as possible. That sign-up form received over three hundred applicants. I was thrilled, but also overwhelmed. It did better than I expected and narrowing it down to twenty-five people (my original goal) was nearly impossible.

So, I got to thinking, if there was this much interest, how many people would purchase the box at cost versus getting it for free? I decided to offer thirty-five boxes for sale on top of the twenty-five original boxes that I was sending out for free to larger book influencers. I sent out a newsletter to the group of influencers that applied and explained the situation.

What happened next continued to surpass all my expectations. I *sold out* of all thirty-five boxes. That was thirty-five additional people that wanted the book enough to pay for it and would potentially post about it on release. Some of them even did! Talk about a win-win situation.

Here is the email I sent as an example of how I converted this cold audience (readers new to or otherwise unfamiliar with me) into purchasing thirty-five book boxes.

Mate Me PR Box

If you're receiving this email it's because you signed up to receive a Mate Me PR box. When I put up this open form, I had no idea how many submissions I would receive or that 15x the number of boxes I'm sending would be requested.

So, without further adieu, I am going to sell half of them *at cost* which means 0% profit to me. What do you get for that? The book, of course, an 8oz soy candle made for this box specifically, an exclusive bookmark, and another 1 - 2 swag items to be revealed.

If you would like to guarantee that you will receive a box, or prefer a hardback over a paperback, please purchase from the above links. There is also the option to purchase only the book, if that is your choice. Or you can choose to not purchase at all and hope you're one of the select few chosen. That's completely up to you. I'm offering this in an attempt to quell my sadness that I can't send out more boxes. In an ideal world, all of you would receive one.

I will reach out in January to let people know if they have received a box. These will likely all be gone by then, since they are also available to my readers.

It's important to keep in mind that book boxes are a lot of work. You need to go into them with your eyes wide open, because unless you're hiring out for it, your time spent is actually the most expensive part of the box. The planning, crafting the box, picking influencers, ordering product, and finally sending it out represent hours of manpower. Don't tell yourself it's going to be easy, because for most people it's not.

You also need somewhere safe to store the products for the time between when they arrive and when you ship out boxes. Not everyone has a basement dedicated to shipping out books. A friend of mine runs Kickstarters, and from start to finish, she busts her butt to have everything out of her house within seventy-two hours of arriving because she simply does not have the space for it. Some people can do this. I am not one of those people. So, consider where you will be storing items and how long it will reasonably take you to ship when deciding to do boxes.

Lastly, limit the number of boxes you're willing to do. Mine was sixty. I prepped beforehand and still spent the better part of a week packaging and sending out. You might be able to do more, you may need to do less, but don't overcommit. If you're unsure how much you can do, I suggest limiting it to twenty boxes, twenty-five at most. This is a good testing number without it becoming too overwhelming.

Reader Signings/Events

The last form of active marketing I'd like to address is reader events. These are conventions and other planned events where you go with the sole purpose of meeting your readers and potentially signing books. Reader events are a great way to cultivate your existing core audience and build up loyalty while also finding new readers. While oftentimes the amount an author spends on an event will not be recouped, they can still be a decent long-term investment of your time—especially for bigger events that will give you more exposure.

An important thing I want to stress is that I wouldn't do reader signings until you hit a certain point in your career. Why? Well, that's a multi-tiered answer. For one, it can be demoralizing if you don't get many readers at your table, which is inevitably the case if you've not built at least some kind of core audience. You might get the occasional straggler who's interested in your pretty covers, but many readers go to signings to buy books they've already read. Another reason is because of time. It takes time and money to plan and attend these events. Until you're at a point that you're making back at least your monetary investment, they can be very draining.

But Kel, when will I know if I'm ready?

To be honest, that's not an easy answer. I attended a convention as a reader before I did as an author to get a feel for events. While there, I had readers that wanted me to sign their books. It was to the point that people purchased books and came to the event (that I wasn't even a signing author for) so that I would sign them because they knew I'd be there. For me, that was my sign from the universe that I was finally ready. It looks different for everyone. I do recommend attending an event as a reader before you go as an author. There is so much that can be learned, from what to bring, to how to set up a table, to simply being able to network with other authors without the pressure of being "on" for readers. That's not to say you need to or even should attend every event before going as an author, but one or two can't hurt.

Important Takeaways

- Active marketing involves you working with other authors or businesses to sell your book.
- Newsletter swaps, BookFunnel promotions, and reader giveaways are great free ways to grow your platform and spread the word about your book.
- Paid promotions like Goodreads giveaways and BookBub are even less effort than free options and yield fantastic results; the only downside is they cost money.
- You can also work with influencers via book boxes and advance reader copies.
- Reader signings can be great for building up your mega-fanbase, but they cost more time and, often, money than any other method.

ADS

Facebook Ads. TikTok Ads. Google Ads. BookBub Ads. Amazon Ads.

The thing all of these options have in common is that you are paying for a space on someone else's platform to tell readers about your books. For that reason, you might think that ads are **active marketing**—and they can be. However, the set-it-and-forget-it nature is also there because you set up your campaign and then probably don't need to mess with it for weeks or months. That has more in common with **passive marketing**.

So, which is it?

My answer is both. Paid advertising can be both passive and active marketing at the same time, or at least have qualities of both.

Now, I'm not going to walk you through how to set up ads, but I do want to address some of the different ways they can be used.

- New Releases
- Sales & Discounts
- Revitalizing Backlists

What do each of these mean?
New Releases

Well, new releases are fairly straightforward. Anytime I have a new release, I run ads for book one in that series. My thinking is, if they've picked up book one and liked it, they're already following up for the subsequent books. It also acts as a reminder for readers to check back and see if there are new books, while also roping in new readers to the series. I see this as more profitable simply because readers like to start at the beginning of a series. If you run your ads to a later book in a series, they have to click through Amazon to go to the first book. It can also create reader confusion. They ask if they are standalones, if they must they be read in order, etc. A confused reader is a reader that doesn't buy. You want to make their job (buying your book) as simple as possible.

Sales & Discounts

Another way to utilize ads is to run them whenever a book is on sale or discounted. This helps get the most eyes on your book while it's at the most appealing price point to readers. You won't make as much per sale, but the idea is that you make more money as they go on to read the rest of the series or other books by you.

Revitalizing Your Backlist

I run ads to my backlist more than any other book, because backlists are where the money is at. But should you run ads to the first book in every series? Probably not. There's a point of contention among authors on whether you should be running ads to your entire catalog versus your bestselling book—even if it's a book you released ages ago. My thoughts? Run ads to the first book in your top two or three bestselling series. Why? Because those books clearly did something right and drew readers in. After all, it's easier to keep a reader than to acquire a new one and it's easier to acquire a new one with the most popular and best-selling product.

My second bestseller was the fourth book I wrote in my career. This book consistently gets the sales and read through. It also brings new readers to my other series because they decide they've enjoyed my writing.

What does this show? If the book sold well when it came out, it never hurts to start pushing it with ads because odds are it will respond better than other, less on-market books. And if you're over here saying, *"But Kel, I've already sold it to sooooo many people that it's hard to reach new ones with ads,"* let me tell you, unless you're JK Rowling, odds are there are TONS of people who have never heard of you or your books before and they're waiting to discover you!

Important Takeaways

- New releases and sales and discounts are good times to run ads where you'd have a set timeframe.
- Backlist ads can be run all the time.
- Always run them to the first book in the series to prevent reader confusion.
- Promoting your bestselling book or series, even if you think you've promoted it to death, is most ideal.

Note: If you're new to Facebook ads, I currently offer a very affordable ads on how to run FB ads in thirty minutes. You can check that out at https:// ruleyourauthorempire.teachable.com.

WHAT HAPPENS WHEN YOU POORLY MARKET?

Let's talk about what happens when you mismarket a book. Maybe a new niche genre emerged and your book has elements of it, so you think, "*Wellllll, maybe I can just tweak the marketing toward this new thing and see what happens.*"

Spoiler alert: Bad things can happen.

By marketing your book as something it is not, you create a negative reader experience. This is because the readers you'll attract are not *your* readers. This leads to bad reviews, which can tank your book, as readers who would otherwise be your readers will now not pick it up.

What's one way to spot if you mismarketed your book?

Poor read through. If fewer than 50% of the readers who picked up book one aren't going on to book two, something went wrong. Whether they DNF'd (did not finish) or simply didn't care to read the next book, you've got a problem. Many times, this can come from marketing the book for the wrong readers, but it could also be from a need to improve craft. One of the reasons it is important to read reviews is so you can suss out the difference. If multiple reviews say the same thing, odds are there is need for improvement.

SOCIAL MEDIA MARKETING

The biggest question I get asked is what authors should post on social media to sell books.

Well, the answer might surprise you.

Logic says that posting about your book with

teasers and character inspiration will be the most effective; however, that's not been my experience. While some posts about your specific book are good, I've found that posting the following are better at getting engagement:

- memes about books
- reading/reader-based posts
- personal life posts that are funny or relatable in some way

That's not to say all your posts should be these topics. However, in posting these things that get readers' attention more, I've also seen a bump in the posts specifically about my books, too.

This is not the only way, and I'm sure there are people that disagree, but the fact is, by posting more algorithm-friendly stuff that people interact with, it teaches Facebook, Instagram, and TikTok that people like your content. That they want to engage with your account. I've had several posts like this go viral and then my follow-up posts about my books get hundreds of responses. This was not my norm previously.

Moral of the story: You can have all the pretty

posts in the world but if they're not converting to followers, it's not effective.

Examples

It's important to keep your posts related to your branding. When I post memes or other content, I keep it related to my books and things that are in them. An author I know who does this super well is Renee Rose. I'm on her newsletter list and one of the recent newsletters she sent out that caught my eye was about her journey with her own sexuality and exploring the kinkier side of life. This was very on point for Renee because she writes spicy love stories. These books almost always have some kind of kink and explore dom/sub dynamics in a healthy way. For her, this newsletter was appropriate branding. If someone wrote sci-fi or thrillers or even young adult romance, it wouldn't be.

Another example I'll give is about an author friend of mine, Coralee June. For the longest time, she wrote whatever genre of romance called to her, but especially dark romance, as it performed best with her readers. Cora changed up her branding to be a romantic comedy author. That's huge, right? Her reasoning for the change was because her books and brand of dark romance didn't really align with her personality or what made her happy. She posted how her family notices she's smiling so much more than she used to, and Cora attributes this to her change in genre. She moved to a genre that better suited her authentic self as a person. Which, given she was always sharing hilarious stories with her readers, wasn't much of a surprise to me. She's always been a woman capable of laughing at herself— and writes love stories. Now her branding reflects that, too.

I challenge you to look at your own social media and ask yourself if your posts are engaging. Do they draw new readers in? Do they get more people to interact with your account? If not, consider using some of these tips to grow your accounts while remaining on brand for you, the bestselling author.

Important Takeaways

- Post content that fits your brand.
- Make sure your brand fits YOU and isn't in conflict with who you are.
- Don't just tell readers to buy your book. Engage with them. This builds reader loyalty, which ultimately leads to them buying your book. Huzzah!

MARKETING WIDE

This section is going to talk about marketing wide specifically, because how you publish HEAVILY influences the best ways to market. The examples given below are some of the most well-known, tried-and-true ways to market your book(s) if you're wide.

- **Making book one free.** This one is great for authors of series, whether they are series that follow the same characters or series of standalones. Free books have always been an effective way to attract new readers and get them hooked on your writing style. As I've mentioned before, if you're going to do this, I recommend using your bestselling series and pushing with that one. However, if you are a new author and do not have a backlist, I do not recommend this. If you've only got a couple of books out, making one free can be difficult to stomach. Wait until you've got at least two books, preferably three, before pushing book one as free or discounted. You'll see more bang for your buck at that point in time.

- **Paid newsletters and other advertising services.** Another way to reach readers is to pay for services like:
- BookBub
- Fussy Librarian
- Bargain Booksy
- Book Barbarian
- ENT Reader News
- Red Feather Romance

These newsletter services often require your book to be discounted or free, but not all of them do. For this strategy, once again I recommend that you have a series with multiple books out before pushing it with these services.

- **BookFunnel Promotions.** This platform offers a place for authors to create and run promotions directly through BookFunnel with fantastic tracking. Many authors specify the promotion is specific to KU or wide authors, which means you can promote with other wide-specific authors to help grow your platforms.

- **Selling direct and running ads to your store.** This one is a fairly new concept, but one I have had great success with. In selling direct from your store, you can guarantee your ads are making their money back *and* increase sales to other platforms. I'll talk about why and how in the next section.

Important Takeaways

- The world is your oyster when it comes to being wide. You have SO many options for marketing. Try them all. Don't be afraid to fail, because it's all learning lessons. Find out what works for you.

SELLING DIRECT

I seriously debated back and forth about where to put this. It's such a huge part of my own platform, but should it go under where to publish? Branding? Marketing? Eventually I settled on marketing because selling direct is an essential part of being wide, in my not-so-humble opinion. If you're going to truly embrace the mindset of selling everywhere, then it stands to reason that you'd sell directly to your audience and cut out the middleman, too.

But first, let's go over what selling direct is. Through the use of Shopify, Etsy, Wix, and Payhip, authors have been creating their own digital storefronts to sell to readers, in addition to publishing elsewhere. This method is a game-changer for wide authors, but it's also got a significant barrier to entry. Due to the time and, oftentimes, monetary investment, I recommend not trying to sell direct until you are successfully making four figures a month.

The Why

Now before we get into how I sell direct, I want to address *why*. You might have guessed based on the previous paragraph that I like the idea of cutting out the middleman, but it goes beyond that. By selling direct to your readers, you're the one gathering information instead of Amazon. You can give them discounts and deals whenever you want. You can even create a newsletter just for the people who are buying directly from you, something I wholly recommend since your regular newsletter is

for people that are used to buying on other platforms and not necessarily open to purchasing direct.

I sell direct because I'm building a relationship with
my readers and like having fewer barriers between
us, which also happens to be fewer barriers between
you and six figures.

The How

There are several ways you can sell direct to
readers, but the main ones I'm familiar with are:

- Wix
- Payhip
- Shopify (I use this one!)

Of these, I've used Payhip and Shopify, but
Shopify is the one I stuck with. Payhip was a lot
easier to set up, but harder to fully customize. It also
didn't lend toward some of the fancier functions
that are must-haves in selling direct, like Klaviyo, a
newsletter service that provides real-time stats on
what your subscribers are buying, how they're
responding to your emails, and separates out
premium subscribers based on their email response
behavior. If you're unsure which one to use,

consider how much traffic you think you'll be doing, what you plan to sell, and then do your research on which platform will best benefit you.

Once you've decided on a platform, the setup can take a little bit of time and work, even if you don't have twenty-nine books like I did when I set up my store. Like with everything else, you'll want your store to be branded appropriately and attractive to new readers. If you want to hire someone, I used AA-CreativeCo to create kelandaureliabookstore.com. If hiring someone is outside your budget, I recommend utilizing YouTube to help yourself learn how to create an attractive site. Once you finish, talk to fellow authors and get real feedback on your store. A great group to do this in is the BABE (Building A Book Empire) Facebook group. It's run by Cameron Snow and Anne-Marie Meyer. They're both great about answering questions and have created a place for authors that sell direct to talk about what's working and what isn't.

Selling

Now that you've done all the setup, I'm going to give you some good news and bad news. The bad news is that you will likely need to redo a lot of it because there is a learning curve. The good news is that if you utilize the right resources, you won't have to redo it a bunch of times.

"Kel, can you just speak plainly?"

Cameron Snow runs a class on selling direct through Author Accelerator. I **highly,** and I cannot stress enough, **HIGHLY** recommend it. If there's anything you should know about me, it's that I've bought or tried most classes out there. I've hired "professionals" that couldn't deliver. Cameron Snow's class is the ONLY class I recommend. Not only does he teach you how to set up your Shopify so it's optimized for selling, he also teaches you how to run ads—and ads, my friend, are the name of the game when it comes to selling direct. There are other ways to reach readers, namely TikTok, but they're not nearly as reliable as ads are. Facebook, in particular, is optimized to help you sell direct. There are certain kinds of ads you can run to reach people who will buy directly from you and even if you know ads, which I did going into the course, there is still so much he teaches, that it's worth the money. When it comes to your author career, if there is one thing after your cover and editing I would invest in, especially if you're selling wide, it's this class.

So do the thing. Even if you have to wait until

you're further along in your journey to six figures, save up and take the class because this one is worth the money.

The last, and perhaps most important, part of selling direct is that it doesn't just sell to readers who will buy at your direct store. It sells your book to *all* readers. What do I mean? When you run ads correctly to your store, there is a percentage of readers that will go and look up your book on their preferred platform and buy from there because it's comfortable. There is nothing wrong with this. Readers are still readers. Money is still money. And selling direct? It's hard.

I won't lie. If you don't have the time to invest into it, don't do it. Half-assing it and then not seeing results is just a waste of what little time you do have, so don't. But if you do, know that it's still hard. Even with Cameron Snow's class. In my humble opinion, he doesn't make it easy, he makes it doable —because I 100% believe the vast majority of people would not come to this and be able to sell successfully on their own.

I'm going to lay down some numbers for you.

My store has a 1.50 **ROI** when it comes to ebooks, not physical editions (this is an important distinction). What does that mean? For every dollar

I spend on ads to my ebooks, my store makes one dollar and fifty cents back. This isn't great. In fact, this isn't even good, in my experience. I'm still new to this selling direct thing and getting the hang of it, and I'm not losing money which is the most important factor to me. So, I accept the 1.50 ROI while trying to scale up. This ROI by itself would be **hard** to make a 6-figure income on, as well as risky.

But you're not just selling in your store. You're selling on Amazon, Apple, Barnes & Noble, Kobo, Google Play, reading apps, and other places. So, while my store ROI is 1.50, when I add in my income from all the other places that my readers go to purchase when they don't buy from my store, my ROI is 3 to 1. That means for every one dollar I spend, I make three. That is doable. Is it the best out there? God no. I know authors doing even better than me, but it is a *viable way to get to six figures*.

And at the end of the day, that is what you're here for, right?

The last thing I want to briefly touch on is physical editions of books, this includes paperbacks, hardbacks, special edition, etc. Unlike my e-book ads, I make 4-8x the ROI on special editions in particular. I have grown my business **substantially** by creating and selling my own special editions. It's too the point that some months my direct store is nearly 90% of my income, and how much I'm making on Amazon and wide retailers doesn't significantly change. If you'd like to learn more about creating and selling your own special editions, I offer a class on just that. You can grab is at https://ruleyourauthorem pire.teachable.com.

Important Takeaways

- There are several ways to sell direct. Pick the one that works for you.
- Selling direct is a time investment. Don't do it if you don't have the time to give it. This is not something that can be half-assed.
- You need a backlist to sell direct. I would say a minimum of five or six books but more than twelve is ideal.
- This is an intermediate-level skill and not something I recommend if you're still getting the hang of other parts of being wide.
- Take Cameron Snow's class. You won't regret it.

MARKETING IN KINDLE UNLIMITED

Kindle Unlimited has fewer options than wide when it comes to marketing. Part of this comes from Amazon's terms of service and part of it is just the nature of the program. I'm going to review the main marketing methods for authors in KU.

Examples

- **Run a Kindle Deal.** *"That's great, Kel, but what exactly is a Kindle deal?"* If you go to the marketing tab on the Kindle Direct Publishing dashboard, you'll find all the ways Amazon offers promotional opportunities and one of those ways is Kindle Deals. You either discount your book or make it free for one to five days total. Kindle doesn't promote this deal, but it does make your book more attractive to readers for a limited time— during which you should be promoting it yourself. Here are some ways to promote Kindle deals:

- You can use a promotional site like BookBub, BookCave,

Freebooksy/Bargainbooksy, Fussy Librarian, or Ereader News Today.

- You can create a BookFunnel promotion and get other authors that write in your genre to join. You can even make it exclusive to Kindle Unlimited books (no wide titles).

- You can run ads on Amazon, BookBub, Facebook, Google, Pinterest, or TikTok (which we touched on).

- You can put together a reader giveaway on social media where you promote your book with other authors who've also discounted their titles. It's highly recommended to choose extremely targeted authors who write similar books to you and whose readers would likely enjoy your work.

- **Run Amazon Ads**. In recent years Amazon has made changes to their platform to make running ads very easy. This is a good and a bad thing, depending on where you are with them. If you're new to ads, it makes it an ideal place to start, but if you've been running ads in other places (Facebook, in particular), this lowered barrier means EVERYONE is running ads. That makes them more expensive. It's because of this that I don't recommend running Amazon ads unless you have a book series longer than four books. Realistically, the longer the better—assuming your read through is good. If your read through is poor (under 50% from book one to book two, book two to book three, etc.), then you're going to have an incredibly difficult time running profitable ads. However, if your read through is good and your series is more than four books long, try them. Thanks to improved metrics, you can see how much of your sales and page reads come from ads on Amazon. This is a great thing, especially when you consider that Amazon isn't transparent about pretty much anything.

Important Takeaways

- Utilize Amazon ads and other programs it offers.

- Paid newsletters and newsletter swaps are still super-viable. You may just want to pick ones that have a KU-based audience.

COAUTHOR MARKETING

Like everything else, marketing looks different when you have a coauthor—and it looks different with *every* coauthor. My partnership with Aurelia Jane is a bit odd here because I handle 90% of the marketing, but don't have to worry about edits. It works for us, but that doesn't mean it will work for you.

Some things to consider when coauthoring are:

- How do you want to split up duties? Will one of you handle all the editing and the other marketing, like AJ and I do, or will you divide them a different way?
- Are you running ads? If so, who is running them? What is your ad budget?
- Will you be doing any reader giveaways? Who is in charge of posting and closing out said giveaways?
- Who will update your back matter for each subsequent release?

- Do you have a direct store with your coauthor? I do, and it comes with its own set of questions, like who will update it? Who will handle email inquiries and technical questions? Who is going to store and ship the books (assuming you sell physical books)?

- How will royalty sharing go at reader events? Will the author attending pay for stock and make all royalties or is there an expectation to share even if both authors aren't attending?

- Who's going to control the SMS sending for each release? What about for promotions?

- Do you have a shared newsletter? Separate newsletters? If it's shared, who is going to write the newsletter? Will they be responsible for answering readers who respond?

What's more, there are questions that go beyond *who* will do something, but *what* they will do, *how* they will do it, and *when* it should be done by.

My suggestion when it comes to coauthor marketing? Look at each other's strengths and weaknesses and figure out the best way to divide and conquer. Be honest about what you can and can't do, and if there are things that neither of you want to do, consider how important they really are. Most things on this list won't make or break you getting to six figures.

Important Takeaways

- Choose a coauthor that complements you.
- Have a contract in place.
- Talk about *all* the things before actually getting into writing. Remember what I said about writing being 30-40% of my job? I have a coauthor and *that's still true.*

Start Ruling Your Author Empire Now

Take a look at your backlist and ask yourself which of these ideas you could implement and try. Make a list, then do one new task a month and track your results. Did you gain new followers or sell more books? That's the measure of whether or not what you're doing is working. This is important in understanding what will move the needle for you.

Once you've done that, look at your next release and ask yourself "What is one new thing I can do?" Test it and see if it makes a noticeable difference in your bottom line or if it was just so-so.

These things are different for everyone, and testing is the name of the game. So, **go forth and pave those roads to your author empire**. The readers (and the money) will follow in time.

CHAPTER 8
CRAFTING THE LEGEND OF YOUR AUTHOR EMPIRE

The final step of the *1 Year to 6 Figures* plan is to craft the legend of your author empire. You aren't just you anymore. You're you, *the bestselling author*. By achieving longevity, other people will come to know you that way, as well. In this section we're going to review some touchstones that help with having a sustainable 6-figure author career. This includes, but is not limited to:

- Series versus Standalones
- Coauthoring and Collaboration
- Subscriptions
- Kickstarter and Special Editions
- Backlist
- Formats: Audio, Translations, Print

- Burnout

SERIES VERSUS STANDALONES

Series. Standalones. A series of standalones. What's the best way to go? Which option will have the most longevity? In my not-so-humble opinion, the short answer is **series or a series of standalones**.

But the real question you should be asking is *why*.

Series are a great way for readers to get invested in a world. It allows them to build deeper connections and those connections are what makes the difference between a good book and that book you recommend to everyone at your monthly book club. You want to enthrall your readers with your characters and world, which is easiest to do with multiple books.

Wouldn't a super-long book do the same?

Maybe…but I wouldn't recommend it. Readers won't pay the price your book is worth if you put an entire trilogy in it. You're better off charging $4.99 for each book than $9.99 for a singular book.

These are reasons why I don't recommend writing a long standalone, versus splitting it into a duology or even a trilogy.

- One, many readers won't pay $9.99 no matter how long the book.
- Two, $4.99 times three books actually yields a higher profit at $14.97.
- Three, it refreshes the algorithm's interest in your books (the algorithm being that of Amazon, Apple, Google Play, Kobo, Barnes & Noble, and any reading apps you participate with).
- Four, it keeps you in readers' minds without having a super-long gap between books.

So how do series help longevity?

This comes back to the third and fourth point I made in the last section. By releasing more frequently, you stay in readers' minds, but it's a fine line. Release too frequently and you can actually see diminishing returns. I probably wouldn't do more than one book a month or less than one book a year. Whatever you choose, try to maintain consistency—both the algorithms and your readers will thank you.

COAUTHORING AND COLLABORATION

Another way you can build up a backlist and extend longevity is by coauthoring or collaborating with other authors. This includes boxset anthologies and shared worlds, both of which I'm very familiar with. This option is especially viable if you struggle with certain parts of publishing or thrive on working with others. If you struggle with marketing, you can find a great coauthor who excels at it. If you are great at marketing but struggle to get the words down, find someone who has an easier time with the words. You have to do what feels right for you, and that starts with evaluating what you need and have to offer.

Coauthoring

Coauthoring is working with another author on a book or novel. There's a lot of ways you can do this and I've touched on a few throughout this book. In this section, I want to talk about the reasons why coauthoring might be a good or bad idea.

Why I Coauthor

My reasons for coauthoring were multifaceted. On one hand, I'm not the slowest writer, but I'm also not the fastest. Being able to release more was the biggest appeal when I started, but it's not actually why I continued coauthoring.

The truth is, I enjoy the process of writing so much more when I work with someone. If you're familiar with CliftonStrengths, I'm Relator number 2. That means I enjoy having deep relationships built on trust—and don't be fooled—coauthoring is a *deep* relationship. Aurelia and I often joke that we're work wives, except it's not a joke. It's true. Coauthoring with someone is not only creating with them, but editing, marketing and, above all, getting paid with them.

Most coauthors have to choose to upload to one person's KDP dashboard and have them pay the other. That requires immense trust. AJ and I share a bank account. We formed a legal partnership between our businesses and have a separate KDP dashboard for all our coauthored books. This also requires trust. No matter how you do it, you need to really know the person you're working with before getting into bed with them.

Protect Yourself (And Them)

This brings me to my next point of order: contracts. I cannot stress enough how important it is to have a coauthoring contract that states:

- The duties of each person
- What happens if either party fails those duties
- A dissolution clause
- Buy-out logistics

These are the main components of a coauthor contract. If you're unsure what else might be needed or if you've covered your bases sufficiently, you can always hop in to my class where I provide a sample coauthoring contract. But I cannot stress this enough: have a lawyer look it over. I am not a legal professional and cannot give you legal counsel. I can only speak from a place of experience and knowledge that I've gained through those experiences.

Why I Enjoy It

Now that we've covered those main parts of coauthoring, I want to loop back to what I was talking about regarding how I enjoy the process more. This is likely because it makes my Relator happy, but in layman's terms for those that don't speak in Clifton Strengths, I enjoy plotting with someone. I like bouncing ideas off another person instead of floundering in my own head, questioning if they're good enough or if there are plot holes I'm missing. I'm a person that's motivated by words on a page and yet I'm not a particularly fast writer, so having someone else that's also getting words in motivates me to get mine in. All of these things would not be possible without a great deal of trust and communication though, so be sure you're ready for that if you choose to try coauthoring in the future.

Boxsets

Boxsets, or anthologies as they're often referred to, are a great way to work with people but not have to invest *too* much into them. For authors that need or want a lot of control, this is an excellent option to pool brains for marketing purposes but still have the final say over your ideas, plots, and manuscripts. I've taken part in several boxsets, most of which were for charity. The purpose of these was to raise money for a specific organization and to gain more readers while at it, but there are a number of kinds that you can do.

For Profit

In fact, I ran a for-profit one where the purpose was to bring in some extra cash while also increasing my base readership. The way mine worked was I picked a theme (enemies to lovers) and invited four other authors to contribute a standalone book to the set. We each promoted the set to our readers through social media and newsletters when it came out. Then, at the end of three months, since this is a limited-time set (and most boxsets are), the anthology collection was removed from Amazon and payments sent. Ta-da! It's actually very simple when running a set for this purpose.

List Aiming

There's one more type of boxset I'd like to speak on and that's a list-aiming set. These anthologies are curated with the specific purpose of hitting a list (*USA Today*, *New York Times*, or *Wall Street Journal*). I've taken part in two of these sets. One was a much larger set that did hit the list we were aiming for. The other was a much smaller one that should have hit *USA Today*, but the list was actually canceled the week of our release, so we weren't able to. Since then, *USA Today* has brought back their bestseller list but with new rules. I'm not very familiar with the changes, as I don't aim to hit it with my books, but you can read up more on it in author Facebook groups like The Author's Vault or 20Booksto50k.

The Basics

If you are doing one with the purpose of hitting a list, there are a few things that you should know and do. The first is that preorders count toward your release week sales, so a long preorder on several platforms is a must. The second thing? Try an exclusive preorder for a while, with Apple in particular. Why Apple? Because currently you need at least 500 sales on two different platforms to hit the list. Amazon is the easy one. Apple is the next largest platform and, therefore, usually the go-to for hitting a list. It helps that they offer promotions if you have a preorder exclusively on Apple. Getting one or a multiple of these could make the difference in the end. After all, you need *roughly* 5,000 preorders to even potentially make the *USA Today* list and there's no guarantees even that will do the trick. I also know people who have made it with just over 4,000, so this number isn't hard and fast. The upside of a list-run boxset, even if you don't make it, is you still stand to gain thousands of new readers and make a pretty penny—and that's what the *1 Year to 6 Figures* plan is all about.

Shared Worlds

The final collaboration method I want to touch on is shared worlds. As someone who has run one successfully for four seasons, I have a lot to say on the subject. First, let's start with the most obvious question many of you are likely asking.

What is a shared world? A shared world is exactly what it sounds like. You create a fictional world that is shared with other authors.

Examples

A shared world could look like having a singular event that all your characters must attend and where they will likely run into each other, like the Monster Ball. This was a shared world that was run by Bam Shepard for several years and operated like an anthology—where they were all offered in one big book, then later could be published independently.

It can also look like creating a literal world where your stories interact, like the Immortal Vices and Virtues Universe (IVV). This is a shared world I created that was incredibly flexible in where the stories could be told, what creatures they used, and even had the option of creating new worlds or supernaturals.

So how was it shared, you might ask?

I required the authors to have at least two cameos with other stories. This meant there had to be at least two incidents where we meet someone else's characters. Most authors did closer to four or five, which worked fabulously, and the books with the most crossovers were often the most successful as well. Some other things I instituted in the IVV world were:

- Since this is a paranormal romance shared world, there was a minimum of one, and a maximum of two, explicit scenes. I did this so that the shared world branding was more defined. Readers love consistency and I wanted them to know what to expect from every IVV book.
- There was a word length requirement. I put this in so that the books were more uniform in nature, and we didn't end up with shorter books getting review-bombed because they weren't as long as larger books.
- There were world rules, such as money didn't exist, people were paid in things like blood, hair, magic-imbued jewelry, etc.
- Books had to remain in Kindle Unlimited for a set amount of time.
- Books had to be priced within a certain threshold ($3.99–$5.99, for example).

- Books could be discounted for a limited amount of time (ten days or less). This was so we kept the series' perceived value higher and didn't have readers waiting for a discount to start reading the books.

They are all things that I truly believe made my world as successful as it was. By the end, we will have over thirty-five books in total that took place in this world, from over a dozen different authors. Many seasons had overlap because authors enjoyed writing in the world so much and readers wanted them to return.

It was a ton of fun and unlike boxsets, I wasn't in charge of gatekeeping money and paying authors when Amazon paid—which was a big thing for me. I loved the idea of working with other people, but managing payments between Aurelia and me was the extent of what I was up for. Designing it where each author was ultimately in control of their own book made my life much easier in a lot of ways because I just had to manage general world questions once contracts were signed.

Everyone knew the terms and conditions up front, and each season got easier as we went along.

Some of that was because the world was already established and some of it was that I learned more as I went.

Time to Shine

The biggest draw that I see for a shared world is the promotional opportunities. Your book is still your own and not being sold with X number of other books like in an anthology, which means it gets its own dedicated time in the sunshine. I personally love this aspect. It lets each author choose their own ad budget and whether or not they want to run outside promotions, while still ensuring a boost from the other authors in the set sharing with all their readers in multiple places.

Marketing Requirements

I do have marketing requirements in my world(s) just to keep things fair. I did this because I noticed that while authors were awesome at sharing in the beginning of a season, they usually dropped off as we went and that wasn't very cool. Some of the marketing requirements look like this:

- Every author must share each new release in a dedicated newsletter.
- Each author must spend a minimum of

$500 on advertisements such as
Facebook or TikTok ads.
- Each author must share each new
release in their Facebook group, if they
have one.
- Each author must share each new
release on all forms of their social
media.

So that's it for my Kel Talk on shared worlds. They can work fabulously if there are very clear-cut expectations from the beginning, but I've seen first-hand how they can fall apart if that's not the case. There's also a very fine line when running one because you don't want to micromanage and be a PITA to work with, but you also can't be too lax and let things fall by the wayside. If you're considering running or joining one, feel free to reach out to me for some one-on-one coaching if you need a sounding board and would like someone to talk it out with before committing.

SUBSCRIPTIONS

When it comes to achieving longevity, few things offer as much support as a subscription-style platform such as Patreon or Ream. While slightly different, both of these offer the opportunity for your readers to pay X amount per month (or year) to you specifically in return for receiving special content. The best part? What this content looks like is up to you.

Example

I'm not as familiar with Ream, but I'm going to deep dive into what I offer on the Patreon I share with Aurelia Jane. We have four tiers.

1. **Team Bandit**. This $7 a month tier gets you access to ARCs, the quarterly short story we write for Patreon, NSFW and SFW character art, audio codes for new audiobook releases, and a first look at pretty much all my announcements—including things like cover reveals, title reveals, first chapters, etc.
2. **Team Nova**. This $15 tier gets you access to all of the above plus work-in-progress chapters, additional voting power, access to my entire ebook backlist, and earlier ARCs.
3. **Team Hades**. This $25 tier gets you access to all of the above, plus 15% off

in our online store, swag sent every
quarter, and a signed copy of every new
release in paperback format.

4. **Team Eres**. This $50 tier gets you
access to all of the above plus a
quarterly box of books delivered right to
your doorstep that includes alternate
editions and special editions.

You can check out my Patreon with Aurelia Jane
athttps://www.patreon.com/kelandaureliabooks.
It's simple and straightforward. It doesn't have a ton
of members yet, but it's also only about seven
months old at the time of writing this book. The
thinking that went into creating this was that I
wanted a place for my superfans that allowed me to
reward them for being there, but also be paid for
my time invested (unlike other forms of social
media). While it's not huge, it follows the wide
author mindset of having as many income streams
as possible and is just one more way that I've
continued to make a healthy six figures.

Some other Patreons that do it even better than
I belong to Navessa Allen, Katee Roberts, and
Harper L. Woods.

Beware

One thing that people do when they start a subscription is overcommit time-wise. You need to be mindful that these are very much a "slow and steady wins the race" proposition. Don't start with tons of tiers. In fact, don't even start with physical tiers. When we first created ours, we offered two tiers that were both digital. Since then, I've added two more tiers because I saw how much physical books were being requested—particularly physical books that were personalized, something that many of my readers ask for but I don't usually offer. So, I created the Eres tier specifically for these people that collect every edition of my books and want them all signed to them. This way, it's a win-win for both me and the reader.

When starting out, calculate how much your time is worth and be sure to put in that amount when it comes to Patreon. That doesn't just mean posting there. It means how much total time you spend for your Patreon writing, packaging boxes, shipping things out, etc.

KICKSTARTER AND SPECIAL EDITIONS

Kickstarter is a crowdfunding platform that's been around for a while but only recently made its way onto the author scene. First, let's talk about what kinds of things you regularly see funded on Kickstarter, such as:

- New Releases
- Special Editions
- Graphic Novels
- Comic Books
- Games
- Audiobooks

This is a pretty broad spectrum and covers all kinds of things from books to stuff that authors don't usually look at, like games. Pretty cool, right?

How this Platform Actually Works

On Kickstarter, the people who support your project pledge money toward certain tiers. These tiers are the rewards you're promising to send out in return for them backing your campaign. At the end of the campaign, their pledge is processed, and you receive the funds roughly 14–21 days later (minus

Kickstarter and Stripe's fees). Are you with me so far?

It helps if you create a profile and back a few projects to get the hang of it on the reader side of things. That way you know how to explain it to your readers when you're on the other side of it as a creator.

To build a Kickstarter you'll want to follow these steps:

1. You need an account if you don't already have one.
2. In the top right corner, you click Start a Project.
3. Once you do this, it'll ask you a series of questions. You need to answer them all truthfully so that Kickstarter knows where to place your project when it goes live.
4. This brings you to the Project Overview page. It's here that you'll get started by selecting Basics.
5. In Basics. you'll give your project a title and subtitle. It's important to use all the characters given to you so that you optimize your campaign for their

search engine. I'll go into this in more detail.

6. Once you've filled in the Basics, you'll go on to the Story. This is where you talk about your project. Be sure to include all relevant information here like: The story — what you're trying to fund. The book(s), aka About the Book, since I'm assuming whatever you're funding is based off your book(s). The tiers. Stretch goals. An About You section. A Why Kickstarter section, where you talk about any experience you might have with fulfilling things like reader boxes or selling direct through your online store.

7. Next, you need to add your Rewards, otherwise known as tiers. In this section you can also include add-ons. I'll go into this more in more detail, as well.

8. Once you've done all of that, you flip to the Payment tab and fill in all the information. It's going to ask you to use Stripe to verify your business. Don't be afraid. It might look complex, but it's actually a very fast process. Once you're

verified, you enter your banking info, and *voila*!

9. Go back to your project review and submit your project for prelaunch. From there, I recommend leaving your project on prelaunch while you fine tune it and promote that page. Once everything is ready, you're good to go for that last step.

10. Hit the big green button and launch your project! Woo-hoo!

It probably sounds really simple how I've broken it down, and it is, but it's also a lot of work. I recommend for your first Kickstarter that you don't overdo it. You're learning the platform, and while you might have interacted with it as a backer before, doing so as a creator is a whole different ball game. Not to mention, fulfilling rewards can be ***very*** time consuming.

If after you've read through this section you're still confused or want to know more, I recommend taking my Kickstarter 101 class. I walk through the process of creating your special editions, setting up your campaign, running facebook ads, and more. If you're interested and would like to know more, go to RuleYourAuthorEmpire.com and click on "Courses".

Case Study: Heather Hildenbrand

An author friend of mine, Heather Hildenbrand, ran a small campaign for her first Kickstarter. She had an overseas publisher print her reversable dust jackets (both sides of the dust jacket are printed) while the books themselves were printed using IngramSpark. This allowed her to not have to bulk invest in 200+ copies of each book up front and store them. Instead, she ordered two hundred copies of each dust jacket and stored those, then ordered the naked hardcovers separately. All she has to do is jacket them and the books are ready to go.

This is a great example of the best of both worlds. Those dust jackets cost less than $3 each. It gave her stock she could continue to sell to readers on her website or at events while minimizing the amount of space and up-front cash required. This allowed her to turn a profit on her campaign, which yielded $8,500 instead of spending it all on books and having to rely on future sales of those books to turn the profit.

Basics

Before we go any further into examples, I want

to double back to the basics. I mentioned that you want to use as many of the characters allowed to optimize your searchability on Kickstarter. What did I mean by this?

To show you, I'm going to use my *Mate Me* campaign. It's my most successful campaign to date and was designed for launching a new book in an existing series of standalones.

Titles

You get sixty characters for the title. Use them smartly. I could have simply named this campaign "*Mate Me*" or even "*Mate Me* Book Box" but instead I titled it "*Mate Me*: A Paranormal Romance Special Edition Book Box." This helped it show up under Paranormal Romance, Special Edition, and Book Box. This, right here, is what I mean when I say to be smart with your words and use every character. Think about what readers realistically search for and optimize your title accordingly.

Subtitle

You get 135 characters for the subtitle and in that one or two lines, you need to explain what your campaign is exactly.

Here's mine: "A discreet limited-edition box of our steamy & hilarious PNR novels. Perfect for fans of Shannon Mayer, K.F. Breene, and Katee Roberts."

This reinforces that it's a book box, but it also tells you what kind of books, in that they are "steamy & hilarious." Next, it uses the shorthand for paranormal romance (PNR). Lastly, it lists other authors who sell books similar to mine. This is a big one, and it's not something I've seen talked about, but I'm convinced it played a part in *Mate Me*'s success. These authors weren't simply chosen because they write similar books. They've also launched their own Kickstarters. That means when readers search their names in the search bar, my own Kickstarter now comes up alongside theirs. This is smart marketing.

Images

The last thing I want to make note of in the Basics section is that you need to have a *good* banner image, especially if you don't have a video. It can have text or just be an image, but whichever way you go, it needs to look ***professional***. It's for that reason I recommend you ask your cover designer to help you. If you absolutely cannot swing it, you can always use Canva or BookBrush to try to design your own. Canva has more flexibility than Book-Brush and can be used for a wider range of things, but BookBrush is easier to use for those of you that are technophobes.

Rewards

The section for your rewards is a tricky one. Similar to Patreon, you don't want to have so many options that it overwhelms you when it comes time to fulfill them.

1. I recommend having a digital or swag reward, since other authors and international backers often want to support you but don't have the funds, or simply don't want the merchandise that's offered in higher tiers.
2. I'd have a tier with just the books (assuming your Kickstarter is for your books and not a game).
3. Then I'd have a tier with the books and swag.

That's it to start with. Three tiers. Grow from that based on how your readers respond and what you learn from fulfilling your first campaign.

Thorough Breakdown of the *Mate Me* Campaign

My base goal for this campaign to fund was

$8,000. Many authors recommend setting your goal much lower, but I diverge in this. Your time is worth money. Your campaign needs certain things like a cover and banner, which also cost money.

Minimum Funding

Now if you don't successfully reach your minimum funding goal, you won't receive any monies, which is why many authors recommend a lower starting goal. But I didn't want to go to the hassle of working with an overseas printer and fully designing these books if this sucker didn't fund and, at a minimum, cover all costs associated with it, plus at least some of my time. You'll have to make your own decision on your campaign funding goal, but at least you can do it with your eyes wide open.

Pricing My Books

The next thing I diverged on is the price of the special editions. I priced these at $40 a book versus the industry standard, which is closer to $60 a book. Why did I do this? Because I wanted to price for quantity. There's a balance to strike between pricing high for fewer backers or pricing low for more. I wanted to find a better sweet spot that helped me optimize getting backers while still maintaining a safe (and significant) profit margin.

Magic Number

In the end, this campaign funded for $40,837 with 296 backers. Of those, over 200 of the backers pledged for physical copies. That's the magic number when ordering from overseas printers. The price per book drops significantly at that point, but you need to have the sheer volume to justify it and not end up with a bunch of unwanted stock in your basement. I say this from experience. Boxes are not an aesthetic, my friend. But they will be yours if you make this mistake.

To my surprise...

When all was said and done and Kickstarter and Stripe took their fees, we received around $35,000 (give or take a few hundred). You need to account for this in your pricing, which I did. I'll be straight with you, though. I didn't think this campaign would do super-well when it first launched. The initial numbers weren't anything to write home about. The biggest thing that made a difference and took us from minimal profits to thousands was ads.

That's right.

Facebook Ads

Kickstarter has the option to sync a Facebook pixel with it. Running ads to your warm audience (readers that have already interracted with your profile) with the use of the pixel makes a massive difference—much like any other kind of launch that you might do.

Let's back up for a second here and address what a Facebook pixel actually is. It's a tracking element that uses code to register when someone purchased or "backed" from a Facebook ad. It's an incredibly useful tool. I plan to shoot a video on how to set up a Facebook pixel for the class that goes along with this book, if you're looking for more information there.

The reason the Facebook pixel is important is because it allows you to track how much you're making from the ads, down to the dollar. That kind of tracking is fantastic and will make your job so much easier.

The "Secret"

I hope this overview of Kickstarter helps you see all the ways you can utilize the many revenue streams available to get yourself to six figures. I wish I could tell you that there's some secret sauce, but I would hope by now you've figured out there isn't.

The "secret" is finding your own way that works for you, whether that means you Kickstart every launch and then put your book in Kindle Unlimited, like I did with *Mate Me*, or that you publish wide and really push your Patreon. There's a hundred—no, a million—ways you can do this, but more than anything, I need you to know that you *can* do it.

I believe in you. What matters is that you believe you can.

THE IMPORTANCE OF HAVING A BACKLIST

A backlist is all the books you've put out up to this point, minus your newest release. That is the technical definition of a backlist. So, what's the reason it's important?

Everyone wants the flash-in-the-pan success. You sell one book, it blows up on TikTok, and boom! Suddenly publishers are calling, and every agent wants you, and all the other authors want to be you—it sounds nice, right?

That's because it's a daydream. A lovely one, definitely, but a daydream, nonetheless. While books do explode this way, it is such a small percentage of what is published. There's no way to ever know if it's going to be you. Even if you write your heart out, use all the Universal Fantasies, all the tropes—it doesn't mean you're guaranteed to be a flash-in-the-pan success. I know, that sucks, but it needs to be said.

The power of the backlist is that it means you don't *need* to be this book.

If each of your books is doing some of the lifting, together they can carry the load. This is a lot less risky and a lot more common for full-time authors.

Why? Because it's simple math.

If you have twenty books that sell $14 a day, or basically three sales per book a day, you get to just over six figures income earned in one year. When I put it that way, it makes more sense, doesn't it?

Now, I need to caveat this statement—it doesn't mean bust your butt and put out a book a month. That goes **against** the work smarter, not harder philosophy I espouse. My first book that really took off in a big way was my fourth book. I made six figures with its release. I show the math simply so it's easy to understand why having more books does help you in the not-so-long-term.

My Takeaway?

I also say this because you want to write the best book you can that is published. I phrase it that way because "best" can throw some authors. Perfect is not published, you guys (and gals). Find a happy medium. Like all things in life, you've got to practice moderation. Write a good book. A book you're proud of. Then publish that sucker, market the hell out of it, and move on to the next one. If it takes off and you become an overnight sensation, then hell yeah! Go you! If it doesn't…that's okay. It's growing your backlist, and your backlist is where the 6-figure money is at.

FORMATS: AUDIOBOOK, TRANSLATIONS, AND PRINT

I'm all about selling the same book in as many ways as possible, so it should go without saying that I'm going to push you to do the same. But before we get into it, please understand I am not saying to go into debt to make any of these happen. That's a bad idea. What I am saying is that it doesn't hurt to squirrel away a certain percentage of royalties every month to save up for print covers, translations, and audiobooks.

Many routes, same math

You know that math we just ran? How twenty books can make you six figures in a year? Well, what if you have five books in one series? It's going to take a hot second to get to twenty books…or is it? If you translated that series into three different languages, you suddenly have twenty books. Same math still applies.

Another example is you take the same five books, turn them into audiobooks—that gets you to ten. Then translate them into two languages instead of three. Bam. Same outcome.

The whole point of this is to talk about the power of offering different formats of the same book. While print is awesome, it's the least likely to make you money out of the three options I talk about. It's also got the lowest barrier to entry since most wraps are $50–100 depending on the designer. Both audio and translations are more expensive, but if you save up over time while writing your next bestseller, they're still doable.

That, my friend, is how you work less and make more.

BURNOUT

The last section in Crafting the Legend of Your Author Empire that I'd like to look at is burnout. *"But Kel, it's not a way to make more money!"*

This is true, young padawan. However, it is incredibly important. In fact, it's right up there with your mindset. The truth of the matter is, I've seen too many authors burn out from overworking themselves. These authors hit a point where the words won't come anymore, and they end up leaving authoring for either multiple years or forever. That's crazy, you guys. We spend so much time, money, and energy on making our passion into our day job that it boggles my mind how people can work themselves to the point they need to quit.

So out of compassion for you, my friend, I'm begging you to please not do this.

Don't skip sleep hours to get the draft done.

Don't miss holidays with your kids to get one more book out, because maybe that one will be "the one."

The only people that are going to remember you worked late in ten years is your family.

So prioritize yourself and the people that matter to you. This career is built day by day, brick by brick. If you're always on the grind, you're never going to be satisfied because there is no end point. It's basically the definition of the journey versus the outcome. So, take care of you, because you're the only one that can.

Longevity can be achieved in a lot of ways, but you have to be in the game to implement them.

Start Ruling Your Author Empire Now

This concludes the section on Crafting the Legend of your Author Empire. I implore you to look at ways you can create longevity for your author career.

1. Sit down and make a list of the things I've discussed in chapters 5, 6, 7, and 8.
2. Arrange them in order of what you're most excited about to least excited about —and start working on the first thing on that list.

I recommend this method because we've talked about so many options that I know it can become overwhelming, but I know you can do this. So, break it down into bite-sized chunks. Pick where you're going to start from, and actually do it.

This is how you'll craft the legend that is YOU.

CHAPTER 9
THE FUTURE OF YOUR AUTHOR EMPIRE

This concludes the *1 Year to 6 Figures* plan in Rule Your Author Empire. If you're saying, *"But Kel, I still have questions,"* don't worry, my friend. I got you. For this last portion of the book, I want to tackle some potential troubleshooting issues you might have.

FREQUENTLY ASKED QUESTIONS

Can I really become a 6-figure author if I have only one book out?

Yes, but I won't lie to you. It's much, much easier if you can get at least two or three books out a year versus relying on one, preferably in a series. Why? I recommend a series for the read through (reading from one book to the next in series) and because you only have to advertise book one. If the book is good, it will sell the rest of the series for you.

Can I make six figures a year from selling in person/at events?

Theoretically, yes. In practice, probably not.

For one thing, these events cost money to attend. For another, you would have to sell a lot of books to make back a 6-figure profit after the expenses associated with the event like table fees and hotel, not to mention the cost of the books themselves from IngramSpark or your printer of choice.

What should I price my book at?

This is a somewhat genre-dependent question. The best way to answer it is to go look at your Amazon categories and see what other books are charging. If that fails, or if you'd like the short answer $3.99–5.99 (for eBooks) is the market average for indie authors currently. Print is a bit wider coming in at $13.99–21.99 for a paperback and $19.99–29.99 for hardback. This depends on your strategy (whether you're charging lower to sell more or higher to account for the percentage bookstores take).

Publisher Rocket is also a great resource to pull this information.

How do I know if my cover is "on genre" and marketable?

Put your cover up next to others in its genre. Does it fit in? Or does it stick out like a sore thumb? Remember, the goal is to be similar but different. If you're having trouble deciphering this, ask a few people (without telling them the correct answer), and see what they say.

Another thing to note is that not all authors in the top 100 of a genre are made equal. If a book says Colleen Hoover on it, it's going to sell, regardless of the cover. That's because those covers are there to prop up the author's name versus the cover selling the book. For us mere mortals, we need our cover to sell our books, not our name.

How do I find reader events?

Getting involved in the community is the easiest

way I know of to really learn about reader events and where to find them. My friends and I send sign-up forms to each other when there's an event happening near one of us that we want the other to attend. I'm sure there are Facebook groups out there as well that keep track of this sort of thing.

I'm going to my first reader event. What do I bring?

That's exciting! And nerve-racking. Rest assured, we've got this. You'll want to bring:

- Some sort of banner, either for your table or a standing one (or both) that has your name on it
- Your reading list is a definite must
- A QR code set up for payment (PayPal, Venmo, Cash App)
- A QR code for where readers can find your books
- A QR code for your reader magnet
- Speaking of books, can't forget those. It's a good rule of thumb to bring twice as many (or more) first in series versus the whole series.

- A price list for your table (it's good to also have QR codes on this)
- Square reader or other credit card reader to accept payment from those not paying via QR code or in cash
- Plastic or wood easels to display books

That's it. Swag is nice but not necessary, and often thrown away. If you feel like you really need it, some of the things I see at signings are postcards, magnets, stickers, pens, bookmarks, and keychains. But again, I repeat, this is NOT necessary, and I would focus on the things that are first.

How important is your title?

This is a loaded question. It's important, but not as much as you might think. The notable thing about titles is that they need to fit in with your genre. So that super-cool, unique title you thought up? Probably not the best fit. Why? Because titles are prime keyword space and keywords are how your book is discovered.

Have you ever looked at the bestsellers in your genre and thought, *"Man, these titles sound similar?"* They do, and that's intentional. Those similar-sounding titles convey to the reader what they're getting into, and that it's the kind of book they enjoy.

How long should my blurb be?

Keep it under two hundred words to stay within the industry standard. Under one hundred fifty is even better. The fewer words you need to hook the reader into buying, the better.

Should I focus on offering additional formats?

I'm all about selling the same product as many ways as possible, so the short answer is YES. Do the audiobook. Get that paperback up. Offer hardcover. Look into translations. These are viable ways to sell the same books you wrote, again and again. *However*, don't put yourself into debt to offer these things. If you don't have the cash now, you can save up royalties from the eBook, or look into working with a publisher for audio or translations.

What should I put in my front/back matter?

Front matter is pretty easy. You have your title page, copyright, table of contents, epigraph and dedication. Back matter usually consists of acknowledgements and your **About the Author** section. You can also include a QR code to a link.tr where you have links to your things like website, social media, newest release, reading list, etc.

RULE YOUR AUTHOR EMPIRE

Well, you did it! You read through the entire book and *hopefully* have been working through the steps of the *1 Year to 6 Figures* plan as we go. If not, that's okay! I'll let you in on a little secret: I also do not do the homework until after I finish the book. I like to take it all in before I start implementing. So, if that's you, now is the time to go back, begin the workbook, and start doing those lessons. You get it as a free download if you join my newsletter at Rule YourAuthorEmpire.com.

If that's not you, however, I hope that you start to see the results that should follow.

After you've done the homework . . .

So how are you doing now? Did the homework

help you begin your leveling-up journey? Reach out and let me know! I want to hear from you. Contact me at kel@kelcarpenter.com or friend me on Facebook!

And if you work through the process faster or want to avoid common pitfalls, you can go to www.RuleYourAuthorEmpire.com and explore the options. I have a course that walks through many of the topics discussed in this book (like setting up ads, Kickstarter, and special edition direct sales etc.). I hope to see you on the flipside.

Go forth and RULE YOUR AUTHOR EMPIRE!

Yes. I have been waiting all book to say that.

CHAPTER 10
RESOURCES

Rule Your Author Empire: ruleyourauthorempire.com

Manifest Your HEA: https://amzn.to/4a1K7jv

Write to Riches: https://amzn.to/3Utna33

7 Figure Fiction: https://amzn.to/3Umjlg2

Trope Thesaurus: https://amzn.to/4bpDzMG

Cover Designer Review Group: https://www.facebook.com/groups/574540393460816/

If This Then That: https://ifttt.com/
repurpose.io

Bestselling Author Next Door: https://shop.skyewarren.com/products/the-bestselling-author-next-door-bundle?_pos=1&_sid=d0cb16cb8&_ss=r
aa-creativeco.com

BABE (Building A Book Empire) Group:

https://www.facebook.com/groups/buildinga
bookempire

Cameron Snow's Class on Selling Direct:
https://authorsaleaccelerator.mykajabi.com/a/
2147617686/3Y8boLke

20Booksto50k: https://www.facebook.com/
groups/781495321956934

Publisher Rocket: https://publisherrocket.com/

ACKNOWLEDGMENTS

There's a few people I need to thank for help making this book a reality. These people are my friends. My partners. My coaches. They cheer me on through the process and make the day to day grind a little more bearable.

The first is my coauthor and best friend who encouraged me to write a book, Aurelia Jane. During a time when I was wanting to give back but not sure how, Aurelia was the voice I needed for guidance (as she often is). I am so thankful to have her as a partner and friend. Keep being an adultier adult, babe.

The next person on this list is Heather Hildenbrand. I don't think I would have actually written the book if not for the additional push from Heather. I was scared to dive into the nonfiction sphere. Fear of failure is a real thing, even though I never viewed failure as an option. This project was different. It was more personal. Vulnerable. I'm laying out all I know on paper and being open to haters telling me it's trash, and that hurts more than when a made up story is reviewed that way. So thank you, Heather, for helping me move past my fears and insecurities.

Perhaps the biggest influence on both me and this book was my coach, Lisa Daily. I started with an outline and a dream. I had no idea what I was doing, but Lisa held my hand through the process. She was my biggest cheerleader and most trusted confidant. I can't thank you enough, Lisa, for the work you put into this book with me. Your suggestions and insights made a world of difference and helped give me the confidence to forge forward. This manuscript is a cumulation of conversations we've had and insights we've shared. I am so thankful to have worked with you.

To my editors Theresa Schultz and Sylvia Mendoza, your changes and suggestions have made this a strong, more readable and therefore more effective self-help guide. Thank you for all the work you put into this.

To my friends, Annie Anderson, Heather Renee, Taylor Poole, and Amanda Pillar—your encouragement has meant the world to me. Thank you for supporting me through the ups and downs of life, from this book to many others, you guys have been there. Keep on rockin'.

Lastly, I'd like to thank you dear reader. Thank you for reading to the end. Thank you for listening with an open mind. I wrote this book because I wanted to make an impact in authorlandia. I wanted to find that person who was like 20-year-old Kel and help her, or him, break into this industry with the knowledge and confidence needed to succeed.

I never gave much thought to a legacy, but in some ways, this is mine for authors everywhere. I hope you take what you need and leave the rest, but most of all, I hope you build the author empire of your dreams.

Until next time,

Kel

Printed in the USA
CPSIA information can be obtained
at www.ICGtesting.com
LVHW091625310824
789777LV00004B/141

9 781960 167736